A Treasury of Canadian Humour

A Treasury of

Cana dian
Humour

Robert Thomas Allen
Canadian Illustrated Library

The Canadian Illustrated Library

McClelland and Stewart Limited,
ILLUSTRATED BOOKS DIVISION
150 Simcoe Street, Toronto 1, Ont., Canada.

PUBLISHER: Jack McClelland
EDITORIAL DIRECTOR: Pierre Berton
CREATIVE DIRECTOR: Frank Newfeld
EDITOR: Leslie F. Hannon
ART DIRECTOR: Keith Scott
ASSISTANT ART DIRECTOR: Hugh Michaelson
DESIGNER: Nick Milton
PICTURE EDITOR: Jane Murdoch
ASSISTANT EDITOR: Walt McDayter
EXECUTIVE ASSISTANT: Ennis Halliday

Co n tents

THE AUTHOR, AS SEEN BY DUNCAN MACPHERSON

Introduction

I'd be a liar if I said I had read all the humour written in Canada in the past hundred years, or in the past ten for that matter, or that I'd even heard of it. The night before I wrapped up this manuscript, I read one of the funniest pieces I'd come across, yet it had been suggested to me only a few days before, and even then I'd put off reading it because of the title, *Lady Chatterley, Latterly*, which sounded too much like some other books I'd read and hadn't liked. I was within a hair's breadth of missing it and I'd bet money that I've overlooked some just as good, and that I'll be told about them, or remember them, the day the printer tells me I can't change anything but typographical errors.

I'm also pretty sure I'll be told about pieces I left out deliberately. Ideas of humour vary greatly, between close friends, between writer and publisher, within families. My wife Helen who has helped enormously in getting this book together, and with whom, by and large, I share the same tastes in humour, was amazed that I was leaving out some essays – particularly some about family life – which she thought were hilarious. Humour is a tricky thing. For instance, almost every writer thinks he writes funny stuff whenever he puts his mind to it. I know writers, good friends of mine, who can give the name and date of little gems of theirs that they've chuckled over, alone, for ten or fifteen years. They produce old yellow clippings of humour they wrote with headings like "The Day I Tried to Open a Tube of Toothpaste," or "Why I Hate Carrots." All writers, including myself, think they've written gassers. Mazo de la Roche, a fine novelist but one whom nobody can claim as a humorist, thought scenes about dogs breaking up picnics were funny, and nobody, including her publishers, could talk her into leaving them out of her books, although they tried.

Some of the selections here I don't think are very funny, but I've included them because thousands of people did think they were funny. On the whole, what I've tried to do is strike a decent blending of what I've laughed at and what most Canadians have laughed at. Usually, but not always, we've laughed at the same things. Some of the best-known humorists have been among the ones I've enjoyed the least, not necessarily because they have had no sense of humour but simply because they've tried to produce too much. I do think it is possible, however, for a writer with no sense of humour to become a well-known humorist, just as, often, the man who gets into the restaurant business is not a good cook. E. B. White, in an essay on humour, quoted one of my own favourite writers, Frank Moore Colby, on this subject, although it seems to me what he had to say placed more blame on the readers than on the writers: "We have praised humour so much that we have started an insincere cult, and there are many who think they must glorify it when they hate it from the bottom of their hearts. False humour-worship is the deadliest of social sins, and one of the commonest. People without a grain of humour in their composition will eulogize it by the hour."

One point that bothers me is the lack of French writers represented here, because it may be misinterpreted as typical Upper Canadian discrimination. (I've already been accused of discriminating against the West, before the book has even been published.) But oddly, the French, who write wittily and gracefully, and are notably more gay and lively than English-speaking Canadians, write very little humour, as such. Besides, humour is almost impossible to translate. What French material I have read (in English translations) doesn't really come under the heading of humour; for example, Roger Lemelin's *The Plouffe Family,* which I thought was one of the best, warmest and most enjoyable books I read.

I've done some editing, but very slight and purely for technical reasons. I've cut out material, but never to my knowledge in a way that has distorted what the author meant to say. All in all I've enjoyed the job and discovered some great reading in doing it. One thing I found in talking to people about this project was, that at some point during the past hundred years, or earlier, Canadians picked up the idea that they have no sense of humour. Today so many Canadians believe it that it approaches a national characteristic. Part of this may be due to Canadian histories which are apt to give the impression that our forefathers never did anything more hilarious than dumping printing presses into lakes, unpacking China tea cups on the Bay of Fundy, or making laundry starch out of potatoes. French-Canadian canoemen are often pictured laughing, but it's a fierce, bearded baring of teeth, and you have the feeling it's just a reflex from getting water in their eyes. Any picture of a typical Anglo-Saxon Canadian in, say, a poster, depicts some clean-cut character with curly hair and biceps like picnic hams who may be smiling, but the impression is that he's smiling at the thought of all that natural wealth of the Precambrian shield and that he's no more likely to really burst out laughing than a moose. Yet the myth of the mirthless Canadian is as unreal as the idea that all Canadians are clean-cut and have muscles. Not even counting a long list of expatriate Canadian humorists – including such famous names as Beatrice Lillie, Marie Dressler, Mack Sennett, the cartoonist Richard Taylor – Canadians at home have produced some top-flight humour.

I didn't find any typically Canadian humour, if my definition of the term is right: that is, a unique *kind* of humour. Some people may feel that if Bob Edwards running obituaries in his Calgary *Eye Opener* for people who never existed isn't unique, nothing is, but it's not uniquely Canadian. It's uniquely Bob Edwards, who happened to be a Canadian, but he would have got as many laughs in Tombstone, Arizona, if he had published there.

As a matter of fact, some of what I consider the best Canadian humour in this book is concerned with subject matter that isn't Canadian at all. I hope nobody will object to it on this account. The ability of Canadian humorists, particularly in the years since World War II, to deal with subjects of universal interest, is, in my opinion, one of the truest indications of Canada's coming-of-age.

If Canadians haven't produced a humour strictly their own, neither have they produced, I'm happy and proud to say, a stock funny figure of a Canadian. Some people regard this as evidence that Canadians are so colourless they can't be caricatured. To me it means we've produced a proportionately small amount of hackneyed, prefabricated humour, the kind that's laughed at because it's labelled "funny." Even when Canadian humour is awful, it just lies there being awful in its own fresh original way.

Pioneer

Days

arly Canadian humour had to be a tough plant to take root among the stumps of Canada's pioneer farmlands and in the mud streets of her towns. Pioneer humour was energetic, home-made, and often depended on liquor. Much, if not all, of the fun found at a barn-raising was due to the grog, which was hoisted to the ridgepole in quantities that would make anything seem funny. Wakes were livened up with liquor. "So hilarious did the participants become," wrote M. A. Garland and J. J. Talman in a study of pioneer drinking habits: "that the corpse was offered a share of the Beverage." The guests at banquets and concerts were often well primed. At a dinner of the St. George's Society in Cobourg, Ontario, there were twelve toasts between the singing of *When I a-Courtin' Went,* and a characterization of Falstaff by the principal of the grammar school, which by then, must have looked pretty good. A lot of pioneer humour depended on what today we'd call audience participation. The chivaree, for instance, which was often played on elderly gents who married young girls. "The chivaree party would steal up to the home of the newly-wedded, usually after midnight," writes the historian Edwin C. Guillet, "and suddenly music from tin horns, horse bells, bull roarers, horse fiddles, tin pans and copper kettles would burst upon the ears of those within the house." Sometimes for an extra belly laugh the boys would climb the roof and plug the chimney with the intention of smoking out the happy couple. "Fighting, and occasionally death, resulted from such proceedings," but, says Guillet, quoting an early commentator, "It was generally considered best to regard it with good humour." Ely Playter, an early Toronto resident, mentions one of these affairs in his diary. It began on Tuesday, was interrupted by rain on Wednesday but started again on Thursday:

York, 12 October, 1802 – Tuesday . . . Capt. Boiton and Miss Willcocks were married this afternoon and the young beaux of the town remindfull of the happy occasion and the French custom of Shivierieing the parties, a number of them in disguise assembled and made a great noise about the old Esquire's house, till the Esquire, his son and Doctor Baldwin came in a great passion with their guns and threatened to shoot if the disguised party did not disperse.

UPPER CANADA ALMANACK FOR THE YEAR 1837.

RADICALS *enjoying* their betting *profits* after the late Ele

PUBLISHED BY
DAVID DWYER, Esq.
TORONTO.

Thirty years before Canada was born, Mr. Dwyer's Upper Canada Almanack was convulsing readers in beards and bombazine. York had recently become Toronto with a population of 9,254, and it could sure use some gaiety. It was the year of the revolt against the straight-laced Family Compact. For many, says historian Arthur Lower, whiskey represented an escape. "The tradition, no doubt exaggerated, was

A FITTING PAIR.

"*Sure such a pair was never seen,
By nature formed to come together.*"

IVES OF THE *SILLY ISLES*,
Or, Marks of Intelligence.

"What are you jumping after there?" said a schoolmaster to an urchin who stood up to his eyes in shirt collar.

"I wanted to spit, sir," was the reply, "and I was jumping up to try to spit over my dickey."

Praise without profit, puts little in the pocket.

Seek till you find, and you will not lose your labour.

that outside every log cabin door stood an open barrel of green whiskey with a tin dipper in it." And to the pioneer humorists, booze was as funny as a banana skin. The amatory efforts of a drunken deacon made risible stuff for the readers of the early Saturday Night. *Towards the end of a wake some wag was sure to belly up to the bier and offer the corpse a drink.*

The Widower Jones, a novel by Edmund E. Sheppard, the founder of the magazine *Saturday Night,* gives some of the feeling of this coarse, ham-fisted backwoods humour in a scene in which the widowed deacon is courting a girl named Ruth. In an elaborate scheme, intended as a joke, although it backfired, the girl's brother gets the deacon on the way to being drunk ("If we're gunto hev fun 'ith th' old fool we may jest as well hev lots uv it"), and the deacon's son, disguised as a visiting Dutch pianist, plants himself where he can spy on his father's love-making.

Wholesome fun like this was accompanied by such written humour as appeared in the *Upper Canada Almanack* for 1837:

> With such a nose and face you dare not look
> In the still lake or in the tranquil brook;
> Or else you're sure to meet Narcissus' fate –
> He died from love of self, you'll die of hate.

OR

> To be let, or to be sold, for the term of her life
> Elizabeth Hall – by the way of a wife:
> She's old and she's ugly, ill-natured and thin
> For further particulars enquire within.

Verses like these were sandwiched between advertisements like:

Dr. M. Souvielle's Spirometer will cure Catarrh, Catarrhal Deafness, Bronchitis, Asthma or any Diseases of the Head, Throat or Lungs.

and, all in all, should make people today happy that they missed the fun and high jinx of the good old pioneer days in Canada.

Nevertheless, it was this rough pioneer period that produced one of Canada's most famous humorists,

11

Thomas Chandler Haliburton, an observant, thoughtful, lusty upper-crust Nova Scotia Scot who began public life as a member of the Nova Scotia House of Assembly. When he was reprimanded by the Speaker for describing the council as "twelve dignified, deeply-read, pensioned old ladies," he resigned, to eventually become Chief Justice of the Court of Common Pleas. In the meantime, he had been writing articles for the Halifax newspaper, *Nova Scotian,* and it was these pieces that were later to appear in book form as the sayings and doings of "Sam Slick."

The casual reader today may be put off by Haliburton's dialect, puns and other devices now fortunately out of style, but Haliburton was doing much more than writing homespun humour: his essays were wry and sophisticated commentaries on Canadian life. He was so popular in England that he outsold Washington Irving and Fenimore Cooper, and for a while rivalled Dickens. He needled the British for their bull-headedness and the Canadians for dragging their heels. Although he had no use for American democracy, his spokesman was a Yankee clock peddlar, a shifty, unsinkable, long-winded 19th Century W. C. Fields. Sam Slick was a shrewd observer of mankind, and many of his sayings, put in modern dialogue and delivered by a method actor, could appear today in *Love of Life* or any of the daytime detergent dramas depicting the desperate state of human nature:

You never seed a small man that didn't wear high-heel boots, and a high-crowned hat, and that warn't ready to fight 'most any one, to show he was a man every inch of him.

If you can get used to the dialect, some of the scenes are as fast-paced as a vaudeville act of the 1930s: for example, the opening to *A Yankee Handle for a Halifax Blade,* a scene between Sam Slick and what used to be called a "dandy," and, later, a "stuffed shirt."

"Well," says he to me, with the air of a man that chucks a cent into a beggar's hat, "a fine day this is, sir."

"Do you actilly think so?" said I, and I gave it the real Connecticut drawl.

"Why," said he, quite short, "If I didn't think so, I wouldn't say so."

"Well," says I, "I don't know, but if I did think so, I guess I wouldn't say so."

Sam Slick, the "shifty, unsinkable, long-winded" clock pedlar created by Nova Scotia's Thomas Chandler Haliburton was more than just funny: his homespun humour was full of hooks. The author was a good judge of men — a Chief Justice of Common Pleas.

"Why not?" says he.

"Because, I expect," says I, "any fool could see that as well as me."

And then I stared at him as much as to say, "Now if you like that 'ere swap, I am ready to trade with you agin as soon as you like." Well, he turned right round on his heel and walked off, a-whistlin' *Yankee Doodle* to himself. He looked jist like a man that finds whistlin' a plaguy sight easier than thinkin'.

In the excerpt that follows, which is from *The Blowin' Time,* Sam gives a cynical account of love and marriage.

This must be an everlastin' fine country beyond all doubt. In winter, when the ground is covered with snow, what grand times they have a-sleighin' over these here marshes with the gals, Natur' meant that season on purpose for courtin'. A little tidy scrumptious-looking sleigh, a real clipper of a horse, and a sweetheart alongside, all muffled up but her eyes and lips – the one lookin' right into you, and the other talkin' right at you – is e'enamost enough to drive one ravin', tarin', distracted mad with pleasure, ain't it? And then the dear critters say the bells make such a din, there's no hearin' one's self speak; so they put their pretty little mugs close up to your face, and talk, talk, talk, till one can't help lookin' right at them instead of the horse, and then whap you both go capsized into a snowdrift together, skins, cushions, and all. And then to see the little critter shake herself when she gets up, like a duck landin' from a pond, a-chatterin' away all the time like a canary bird, and you a-haw-hawin' with pleasure, is fun alive, you may depend. In this way Bluenose gets led on to offer himself as a lovier, afore he knows where he bees.

But when he gets married, he recovers his eyesight in little less than half no time. He soon finds he's treed; his flint is fixed then, you may depend. She larns him how vinegar is made: "Put plenty of sugar into the water aforehand, my dear," says she, "if you want to make it real sharp." The larf is on the other side of his mouth then. If his sleigh gets upsot, it's no longer a funny matter, I tell you; he catches it right and left. Her eyes don't look right up to his'n any more, nor her little tongue ring, ring, ring, like a bell any longer; but a great big hood covers her head, and a whappin' great muff covers her face, and she looks like a bag of soiled clothes a-goin' to the brook to be washed. When they get out, she don't wait any more for him to walk lock and lock with her, but they march like a horse and a cow to water, one in each gutter. If there ain't a transmogrification it's a pity. The difference atween a wife and a sweetheart is near about as great as there is between new and hard cider: A man never tires of puttin' one to his lip, and make plaguy wry faces at t'other. It makes me so kinder wamblecropt when I think on it, that I'm feared to venture on matrimony at all.

– *The Clockmaker,*
Thomas Chandler Haliburton.

Fifteen years before Haliburton, Thomas Mc-Culloch, a Scottish-born Presbyterian clergyman, was writing criticisms of local morals for another Halifax paper, the *Acadian Recorder*. McCulloch's pieces, which were really practical sermons on how to get along in life, caused a tremendous stir, with their fascinating gallery of characters – Driddle the fiddler, Israel Doublerib (who wore out two wives), Peter Pumkin and his large family of daughters "the most noted bundlers in town," Loopy, a shiftless forerunner of the American comic-strip Yokums of Dogpatch, who even had a son called Abner.

Loopy lived then, as he does now, in a little log hut covered with spruce bark. Neither the outside or inside of it, I recollect, presented any inducement to visit it twice. His door was always beset by a couple of starved pigs, which occupied this station for the double purpose of enjoying the benefit of the puddle, and of being at hand to make good their entrance when the door happened to be opened. Mrs. Loopy was frequently from home, and required to be dressed. On this account the eating apparatus was not much looked after. They usually stood upon the table, amidst scraps of pork or fish and piles of potato skins; of which, also the chairs had usually a proportion. As for the bed, it was in constant use; and served the whole family. In Loopy's it was a standing order, that the dog jumped out, and Loopy and his wife jumped in.

One of the most peculiar writers in the Maritimes during the mid-1800s was James de Mille, an unsuccessful bookstore proprietor of Saint John, New Brunswick, who became professor of classics at Acadia College, then professor of English at Dalhousie, and as a side-line turned out fiction at the rate of 30 books in less than 20 years. Although born just

37 years after Haliburton, there was little if anything in his writings that pertained to pioneer life. He wrote novels with romantic, involved, incredible plots that touched Canada only incidentally. The *Lady of the Ice,* for example, although it takes place in Quebec City, could have taken place in Charleston, South Carolina, and the lady could have had bloodhounds snapping at her instead of being beset by blizzards, without altering anything essential to the story. De Mille wrote for money and he's unique in that, to today's reader, he is sometimes as funny when he isn't trying to be as when he is:

I raised her in my arms. I supported her head on my shoulder. The storm beat pitilessly; the stinging sleet pelted my now uncovered face. All my thoughts were turned to the one whom I held in my arms. I took the cloud which was wrapped around her head and tenderly and delicately drew it down from her face. Oh, Heavens! what was this that I saw?

HEARTS AND FLOWERS

When we formed the idea of offering Canada a literary wreath, we determined that the only hands which should weave this garland should be those of her children by birth or by adoption, and that no flowers, however lovely, should be twined with the "Maple Leaf" than those that blossomed amidst her forests.

– A preface to the *Maple Leaf* or *Canadian Annual,* a Literary Souvenir for 1847

The above paragraph could stand as the editorial policy for this book, but it's included here as a specimen of the kind of prissy prose people wrote during the mid and late 1800s. It was a time not only when pieces of journalism were called "wreaths" and "garlands" and "flowers," but when a turkey's breast was called its bosom, and women pretended that they stopped at the waist and began again at their ankles. Men, in many respects, pretended that women didn't exist at all, and excluded them from humour as from everything else more worldly than doing down pickles. While the women bustled around preparing dinner, the men gathered behind closed doors in the parlour to snap their braces and fracture themselves with the latest jokes. Or they sat out on the farmhouse veranda telling jokes about the barn-yard bull, an animal that seems to have had as great a fascination for early Canadians as for the people of

ancient Crete, although early Canadian women not only didn't tell jokes about it but also refused even to name it, referring to it simply as "the animal." In ordinary social levels, no man would tell a bawdy joke to a woman. Women wouldn't tell one to anybody,

and rarely a joke of any kind. In public, the rule was a prim and ladylike decorum, although in private women could, and did, collapse in mirth recalling some pratt fall of the lordly male, probably having visions of the shape of things to come.

Yet, underlying the world of refined elocutions, coyly ruffled piano legs, stereoscopes, sentimental art and extreme gentility, which we usually refer to as "Victorian" was a morality that wasn't at all "Victorian," along with a national sense of humour that hit an historic low. Canadians got their fun out of lobbing verbal rocks across the U.S. border, and treating members of every race but Anglo Saxons as comic valentines. James De Mille, who was well travelled and wrote a series of articles on Europe called *The Dodge Club Stories,* a forerunner of Mark Twain's *Innocents Abroad,* had foreshadowed this by using people of foreign lands as comical props. One of his characters keeps shouting "washy, washy!" to an Italian landlady whom he wants to take care of his laundry.

"Me . . . want . . . you know . . . me . . . gentleman . . . me want to tell you this. Clothes . . . you know . . . washy . . . washy . . . washy. No, no, not washy, but *get* washy. My clothes . . . I want to get them washed . . . laundress . . . washy . . . soap and water . . . clean 'em up . . . iron 'em . . . hang 'em out to dry."

In Ingersoll, Ontario, Canada's "cheese poet" James McIntyre was turning out poetry that he didn't intend as humour but which has become funnier with the years.

SHELLY

We have scarcely time to tell thee
Of the strange and gifted Shelly
Kind hearted man but ill fated,
So youthful, drowned and cremated

BIRTH OF CANADA JULY 1ST 1867

Hail Britannia's noblest daughter
Who is surrounded by the water
Of many a lake and broad sea
Land of beaver and of maple tree

But what really stirred McIntyre was the cheese industry of Oxford County in Ontario. His most famous, or notorious, poem was written to commemorate Canada's first big cheese, which weighed 7,300 pounds and was photographed with 19 people sitting or standing on top of it. McIntyre wrote a six-stanza poem beginning:

> We have seen thee, queen of cheese,
> Lying quietly at your ease,
> Gently fanned by evening breeze
> Thy fair form no flies dare seize

which, oddly, didn't prevent the cheese being sold to a buyer in Liverpool, England. Another poem that has earned for McIntyre a kind of immortality, is entitled:

OXFORD CHEESE ODE

The ancient poets ne'er did dream
That Canada was land of cream,
They ne'er imagined it could flow
In this cold land of ice and snow,
Where everything did solid freeze,
They ne'er hoped or looked for cheese.

A few years since our Oxford farms
Were nearly robbed of all their charms,
O'er cropped the weary land grew poor
And nearly barren as a moor,
But now their owners live at ease
Rejoicing in their crop of cheese.

And since they justly treat the soil,
Are well rewarded for their toil,
The land enriched by goodly cows
Yields plenty now to fill their mows,
Both wheat and barley, oats and peas
But still their greatest boast is cheese . .

To us it is a glorious theme
To sing of milk and curds and cream
Were it collected it could float
On its bosom, small stream boat,
Cows numerous as swarm of bees
Are milked in Oxford to make cheese . .

A series of humour magazines that appeared in the 1800 s – *Grip, The Moon, Diogenes, The Grumbler, Grinchuckle,* and others – turned out some of the worst humour Canada has ever produced, at least it seems the worst now although it was funny to Canadians at the time. Most general magazines of the day went in for topics like the emigration of the Mennonites, Home Rule for Ireland, Darwinism, good manners, anti-Bloomerism, answers to biblical questions and Manitoba's abolition of separate schools. In his *History of Canadian Magazines,* Noel R. Barbour says of the *New Dominion Monthly,* which was founded a month after Confederation, "There was nothing more frivolous than the rules of lacrosse." But although the average magazine was relentlessly serious, the humour magazines were relentlessly funny, which was even worse, particularly in view of the brand of humour that was in vogue.

Our grandfathers and great grandfathers chuckled over a kind of anti-Americanism that would make today's anti-Americans seem coldly objective. *The Moon,* published on Adelaide Street in Toronto, announced that it was being published "with the object of supplying Canadian readers with satire and humour dealing as much as possible with Canadian subjects . . . without being under an obligation to Uncle Sam for it," then forgot Canada entirely and launched into a tasteless and pointless tirade against American girls:

The American Girl No. 1, the Society Girl, shows a frightful scoop-nosed creature stretching chewing gum, accompanied by the following verse:

For Son-in-law

Sweet Sylvia, how your pa does slave
To trap with cash some noble knave—

Sweet Sylvia with the winking eye,
And teeth just built for biting pie—
And chewing gum

Jl. I. TORONTO, AUGUST 23rd, 1902. No. 13.

Price 5 Cents. $2 Per Annum.

In 1972.

Visitor from the Province of Pennsylvania: "Who are these curiously dressed old men I see in your streets?"

Fair Ontario Girl: "Oh, they are some of the Canadian Mounted Rifles who returned from South Africa in 1902."

The Moon, *like the other funny mags of the Victorian era, rated minorities (and convicts) as worth a giggle.*

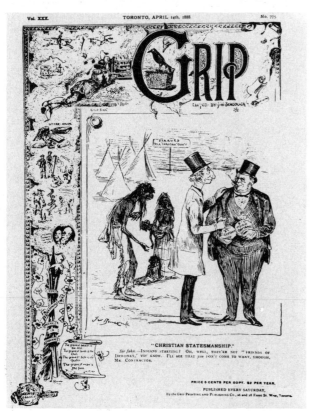

Vol. XXX. TORONTO, APRIL 14th, 1888. No. 775.

"CHRISTIAN STATESMANSHIP."

Sir John.—INDIANS STARVING? Oh, well, they're not "FRIENDS OF DEWDNEY," yo' know. I'll see that you don't come to want, though, Mr. CONTRACTOR.

PRICE 5 CENTS PER COPY. $2 PER YEAR.
PUBLISHED EVERY SATURDAY.
By the Grip Printing and Publishing Co., 26 and 28 Front St. West, Toronto.

Grip *was founded by J. W. Bengough, a cartoonist who advocated prohibition. He wrote The* Gin Mill Primer.

The idea of an American dressing up, attending a ball, or pretending to be civilized in any way seemed to strike Canadians as unfailingly hilarious. In May 5, 1860, *The Grumbler* published a satire, called
"EUPHEMIA, Or The Stricken Heart:
A Story of Fashionable Life in
New York.

Gracefully, oh! how gracefully did the lovely Euphemia St. Jullien glide through the dance that night. The glorious creature moved with that proud and swanlike freedom known only to women whose infancy has been swaddled in the star spangled banner. The costly velvet carpet (from Bulby & Bucks, 169 Broadway) scarcely yielded to her white satin slipper as she skimmed along.

The Honorable Jefferson F. Kidoodle watched her with a lover's intense gaze. Already he had distinguished himself in the field and in the council and though he looked delicately feminine, those who glanced at his rose colored vest might see between it and his richly embroidered shirt a silver handled bowie knife.

"Pretty lady," he said, in the rich sweet voice peculiar only to the Italian and the American, "may my devotion aspire to a spin with you?"

Readers of humour magazines in Victorian days thought Chinese, Catholics, Jews, Germans, Dutch and Americans were funny. English-speaking Canadians thought French Canadians were funny because of the way they spoke English. Convicts were funny and so was anyone with a physical disability. *Punch in Canada* frequently referred hilariously to his hunch back, "Last week I took my hump to Kingston." The use of dialect was frightful. The *Epistles of Hugh Airlie,* a pamphlet published in 1888, was about as long as this book and entirely in almost unreadable dialect. This rage for dialect is often combined with pointless misspelling. An item in *The Grumbler,* March 20, 1858, to someone in an Australian penal colony begins with a letter: "Dear Arthur: I suppose that in yure pakuliar situation you do not hear much noos. O since that time in 1858 when you took your first pleasure trip at the expense of the Guvernment how mutch has been going on in these 4 years Canada has bekum Independent." An article in *Diogenes,* a humour weekly published in Montreal, goes on interminably with such stuff as "I 'ad almost thought a fortnight ago as I'd never be able to 'rite no more fur I war a meltin' away by the hinch with the 'eat." It wasn't only in the East that humour had reached this low point. Out in British Columbia things were just as bad. In the *Cariboo Sentinel,* May 6, 1871, a letter began:

CHARLES AUGUSTUS SIMMON ON KONFEDERASHUN

Feb. the Oneth. in the year A.D. 1871

Mr. Ulyses S. Grant, Esq., President of the United States, Boss and Chief Cook of the Iland of San Dominoingo, Kyng of the Kanible Llands, cetry, cetry May it pleeseth ure Ulysus-ship –

I, Charles Augustus Simmon and brother, & our wives, the people of Kanaday, in parleyment gathered together (& agreeing together, which am a rare kermodity in family cerkles) not being of sound mind but perfekly Krasie and not havin the feer of stars & stripes b4 our ise, du in our wisdum ofur this peteshun fur the kinglomorisashun of awl Ameriky, and 2 place it under the soul guvernment ov that burd of pray kalled by geologists the Amerikan Egal.

Punning was relentless. Once a Canadian of the era got an idea, he drove it right into the ground. "If you have a child and beat it, how does that prevent it from having small pox?" asks *Grip*. "Because you whacks and hates it." (If you don't get it, don't worry. *Grip* nails it down with a solid clout, explaining, "vaccinates it.")

Before the turn of the century Canadians could laugh at things that today would have us organizing protest marches:

There is a report current in the English newspapers that flogging has been abolished in several of the Public Schools. If this statement be true, *Diogenes* deeply regrets it, for he conscientiously believes that the birch is the fundamental branch of knowledge, most needed in all boys' schools. His advice on the subject of the education of the young has ever been – stick them to it. You must *cane* a boy occasionally if you make him *able*. The rod is a means to be applied to *an ènd*. These maxims will be found invaluable. *Diogenes* treats with cynical contempt the assertion that corporal punishment makes boys dull and stupid. Nay, more. He is content to refer this point to the boys themselves, who, one and all are prepared to make affirmation that a moderate use of the cane invariably makes them *smart*.

– *Diogenes*
November 20, 1888

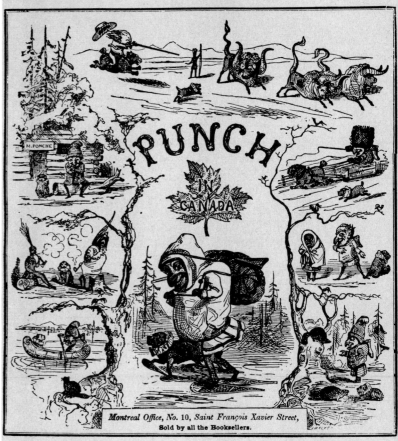

Vol. I.—No. 20.] **October the 20th,** [PRICE, 4d.

PUNCH IN CANADA

M. PONCHE

Montreal Office, No. 10, Saint François Xavier Street,
Sold by all the Booksellers.

THE GRUMBLER.

NEW SERIES—VOL. I. TORONTO, SATURDAY, MARCH 31, 1860. NO.

THE GRUMBLER.

" If there's a hole in a'your coats
I rede you tent it;
A chiel's amang you taking notes,
And, faith, he'll prent it.

SATURDAY, MARCH 31, 1860.

GRUMBLES FROM QUEBEC.

To an Enlightened Public.

As patriotism is the last resource of a scoundrel—so a government office seems to be the last resource of a ruined man. It matters not whether a good man or a bad man—whether he ruined himself, or was obligingly ruined by others, he lays himself down at the feet of ministers, fawns, wheedles, flatters with forty-thousand devil-power. And for what? That he may become the servant of an ass, the drudge of a dunderhead, the scrivener of a blockhead clerkocracy—doing dogs' work for dogs' wages. Aspiring after such a noble prize Quebec contains a noble army of martyrs, who cry "give, give" with more than ordinary avidity, and "grab, grab" all they can get with more than swell-mobsmen eagerness. But why quarrel with them. They must make their bread and butter at somebody's expense. Why not at the expense of the disgusting public? Everybody preys on the public from the youngest novitiate in the appropriating-other-people's-handkerchiefs-to-one's-own-use fraternity to the oldest member of that taking-money-out-of-other-people's—

A Mere Rumor.
—Some say that the H. R. H. the Prince of Wales will bring out with him a limited number of (K)night-caps. A Power of Attorney will doubtless be given to him by Her Majesty, to fit them on deserving Canadians, in her name.

N. B.—We prefer calling them (K)night-caps, though some term them (K)night-hoods. The old name is the better one.

THE FASHIONS.

Spring has come bringing with it bright skies and sunshine and the usual display of new dresses, bonnets, and gay ribbons. Its approach is not by means unknown to the gentlemen either, for appear in fancy coats, fashionable trowsers and caps and hats. We shall first notice the effect on the ladies attire. Those graceful jaunty little still retain their place in the ladies' affections, formerly, head the list. We, if we know our own ings, adore them, and are ready to kiss every pretty lady that wears one. If any lady choose to take up, she will find us by calling at our rooms, 21 Norfolk Buildings, Toronto. Ladies in the country may communicate by letter prepaid.

As we were observing, whenever we see a pretty lady with a hat sitting jauntily on her head, our eye front expands and we find it hard to restrain our feelings. But when in addition we watch a glimpse of a young lady with a pretty hat, covering beautiful gracefully hung in a pretty fishing net, we have to round the nearest corner till the fair one has passed. Hoops—ah—yes—hem !—bless our heart—we nearly forgetting Dame-fashion-witchcraft. Hem ! Crinoline, we should say, is nearly as large as her ! but its an old subject. There is no use When the ladies take a notion into their heads can get it out. There is, absolutely, no use saying thing about it.

As to the other parts of a lady's spring attire not speak advisedly as we are not a lady. If we should be able to give a great deal of useful tion. As it is, and as these are hard times, we advise the ladies to make up their old dresses—

Diogenes *magazine was at ease with puns "You must cane a boy occasionally if you make him able."*

Many jokes and humorous essays are baffling to a modern reader: The following is an item from *The Moon,* complete and unabridged, unqualified and unexplained:

Mrs. S. Lobb received at her beautiful new home on Pear St. on the 4th, just after her return from her wedding tour. The bride was dressed in her bridal robe of cerulean satin velvet cheese cloth, with a train of fancy striped trousering to match the stair linen. The bodice was cut on the bias and fastened to the skirt somehow. She wore a double string of real imitation pearls, the gift of the bridegroom. She had four molars and two incisors fitted with genuine Sicily cement. The dining-table was draped with full fawn-colored fila-gree. The silverware was all genuine German cut. The limbs of the table were covered with cream-colored cottonade. The refreshments included pomme de terre grasse, cooked en robe de chambre and lait de beurre churned the day before. The wine included liqueur au gingerubre and eau de deltz, plain. The gentlemen all wore neckties, socks and canes and smoked Stonewall Jackson cigars, Colorado maduro, regular 5¢ straight, or 7 for a quarter.

I've tried, until I've nearly gone cross-eyed to find humour in these publications, but haven't yet, and I reached a point where I refused to read any more of the fine print. One of the associate editors of *Grip* was Phillips Thompson, later one of Canada's finest journalists, and a foreign correspondent for the Toronto *Globe*. He became a spokesman for the Irish tenant farmer, and a dedicated fighter for the under-privileged. A tribute was paid to him in *Adventures of a Columnist* by Pierre Berton, his grandson. It was a just tribute, but when Phillips Thompson was being funny, he wrote the same awful humour as everybody else wrote those days and it's significant that, as Berton says, "he reached the heights of success as a humorist." I looked at some of Phillips Thompson's old humour pieces and, judging by the tales told to me when I was a kid, I think my own grandfather, who owned a small roofing business and never wrote anything, was funnier. In *Moon,* Thompson wrote a five-stanza poem, starting:

> Inter bisness ez a sage
>   I seem goin'
> Ez my wiskers wite with age
>   Keeps a-growin'
> Wen folks pass the time o'day,
>   "Uncle Jed," they often say
> "How'll the weather be terday
>   You'll be knowin' "

These magazines relied largely on a kind of humour I don't find any funnier today than it really was 100 years ago. It's the kind in which the writer gets an idea, say, of making Noah into an Air Canada pilot, then goes on for a thousand or more words without having any new ideas, but just developing the first one (e.g., having Noah do things like making announcements of flight times to the animals in the ark) I think it's the laziest kind of humour and I should know. I've written it myself when I was tired and broke.

WESTERN WHOOP-UP

NOW SHOWING ON THE INSIDE

Bob Edwards'
Summer Album
EYE OPENER
Robert W Service

As Canada approached the 1900s, a new kind of humour came out of the West like a fresh mountain breeze. *The Ledge,* a paper published in New Denver, B.C., ran a masthead that was right to the point, showing a bulldog eating a delinquent subscriber.

The Ledge has never been raided by the sheriff, snow-slided by cheap silver, or subdued by the fear of man. It works for the trail blazers as well as the bay-windowed and the champagne-flavored capitalist. One of the noblest works of creation is the man who always pays the printer, he is sure of a bunk in paradise, with thornless roses for a pillow by night, and nothing but gold to look at by day.

– R. T. Lowery, Editor and Financier

Lowery's paper had the flavour of a mining camp. Drink was dealt with as a fact of life, not just for characters in jokes, but for everyone, including the publisher.

In crossing the Fraser River coming from Chilcotin, Jack McInnes, a stage driver, says that he saw a fish sixty feet long which he thinks must have been a sea serpent. It must have been a floating tree, for the whiskey along the Cariboo road is not strong enough to raise fish of that length.

Current events and issues were reported in a blunt outspoken personal style:

The Doukhobors are out on another hunt for Christ. They are roaming about the Saskatoon country half-naked and starving. However ignorant they may be, they know enough not to look for him in B.C.

But the man who really jolted the 1900s with his new brand of journalism was Bob Edwards, a stocky Scot with a straggly moustache, who drifted to the Canadian Prairies in 1895 after a spotty career that had taken him to the French Riviera and to an Iowa farm. He came to Winnipeg, then heard of opportunities further west. He began publishing in Wetaskiwin (Sixteenth Siding) Alberta, and thereafter published wherever he lived – in Leduc, Strathcona, High River, Calgary. He was the most famous floating publishing venture Canada has produced. He was a dedicated drinker, and published between binges, writing his whole paper himself, in long-hand. His *Calgary Eye Opener* became known from coast to coast, in both Canada and the United States. Towns took sides for and against him. His columns were chuckled over in bars, brothels, and, more or less furtively, in thousands of respectable homes throughout the country.

Edwards was able to sit amusing himself with nonsense; for instance, writing a caption for a headless underwear ad, "Charles I, after his execution." Yet Edwards would tackle anything or anybody on what he considered an important issue. During the First World War years, he ridiculed Canada's Minister of Militia, Sir Sam Hughes, with captions for a sketch of a statue showing a man on a charger, "General Sir Sam Hughes Giving his Sermon on the Mount," "Sam Hughes Commanding the Sun to Stand Still." He campaigned against the C.P.R. for safer crossings and when R. B. Bennett, later Prime Minister of Canada, and at that time a C.P.R. lawyer, banned the *Eye Opener* from the line, Edwards ran pictures of C.P.R. wrecks, or, which was just as bad, announced "there were no C.P.R. wrecks this week." Over one caption "Another C.P.R. wreck," he ran a picture of R. B. Bennett. He took legal chances just the thought of which would turn a modern publisher pale. Lord Strathcona, in England, learned, in a towering rage, that, according to a report in a Canadian paper, The Calgary *Eye Opener,* he, Strathcona, had delivered a glowing tribute to a horse thief named McGonickle. He threatened to sue, but didn't. Another time, Edwards called himself a liar in print and threatened to sue himself, and so confused the Premier of Alberta, who was considering suing Edwards at the time, that the Premier gave up the idea.

Edwards had a natural wit. He rocked Wetaskiwin

THE EYE OPENER.

Vol. 5. No. 48.   Calgary, Alberta, Saturday, November 10, 1906.   Price Five Cents.

50,000 CLUB for CALGARY!

WANTED. Crooks, Confidence Men, Gamblers and Thugs, Protection Guaranteed by the Police at Reasonable Rates. Apply to Secretary Board of Trade, Burns Block, Calgary.

with a report on a town council meeting at which a debate had been held about what size cemetery the town needed. Edwards cracked. "Ten acres – five for each of the town's doctors." When R. B. Bennett, with whom Edwards eventually became friends, invited him to attend a political banquet, then asked Edwards to say grace, Edwards replied, "If you don't mind, I'd prefer that the good Lord didn't know I was here."

The Calgary *Eye Opener,* was published from 1904 to 1922 and sold for a nickel. It is estimated that five hundred issues were printed. It reached a circulation of 30,000. Edwards said he began his publishing career with $1.47 and ended it with 67¢ and a half bottle of whiskey. Selections from the *Eye Opener* were published for three years in a book called *Bob Edwards' Summer Annual.* An ironic twist to Edwards' career was that, after publishing probably more humour about drink than any publisher before or since, he turned against it, quit drinking, and came out for the drys in the temperance elections of 1915.

THE PASSING OF PETER MCGONIGLE
by Bob Edwards

It is with unalloyed grief that we record the untimely death of Mr. Peter J. McGonigle, editor and proprietor of the Midnapore (Alta.) *Gazette.* This also means the demise of the *Gazette.* While examining an ivory handled revolver which the bartender of the Nevermore House had, during the editor's absence in Port Arthur, accepted from a stranger in lieu of payment for a two-day drunk, the weapon unexpectedly went off and lodged a bullet in Mr. McGonigle's abdomen. A physician was hastily summoned by phone from Calgary. In the meanwhile, Jimmy, the bartender, summoned help and had his old friend gently raised from the floor and stretched out on the bar with his head comfortably resting on the slot machine. Mr. McGonigle retained consciousness, but complained of great pain. A tumbler of brandy eased his sufferings somewhat, but he whispered to Jimmy that he feared he had been sent for at last. The tender-hearted mixologist thereupon threw another tumbler of brandy into him, after which as soon as it had percolated through his system, Mr. McGonigle declared himself as feeling much better.

Pending the arrival of the doctor from Calgary nine miles distant, Jimmy did all he knew to staunch the flow of blood. Ripping open the shirt and locating the spot where the bullet had entered, he took the glass stopper from a Gooderham and Worts flask and inserted the blunt-pointed end into the hole, keeping it pressed down with his thumb to stop the rush of blood. The contents of the flask he absent-mindedly poured down his own throat from time to time. One of the men took Jimmy's place holding down the glass stopper while that worthy prepared a round. At someone's suggesion the slot machine was taken from under the wounded man's head as being too uncomfortable, and the cash register substituted. In lowering Mr. McGonigle's head onto the keyboard they rung up $14.95 but P.J. said it was a great improvement on the slot machine and added that he hoped the Doc wouldn't be long as he felt himself getting awful weak.

An auto suddenly pulled up in front of the Nevermore House and out jumped the looked-for doctor carrying a small black case.

"What room is the man in who was shot?" he curtly inquired of the men gathered in the office.

"He's in the bar," was the response.

Mr. McGonigle, on the approach of the doctor, turned his head, ringing up $1.40 in the effort and greeted the doctor with great cordiality, insisting upon his having a drink before making his examination. Then everybody but Jimmy was ordered to "get out and stay out."

As the doctor bent down to examine the wound, Jimmy gave a pathetic little grin and explained that it

23

The Three Boozeketeers

would have taken too long to whittle a cork into shape. The doctor's face grew grave.

"The bullet must be located and extracted," said he, "and he will have to be taken to the hospital in Calgary by the first train."

"I will hurry back in my car and arrange for a ward in the Holy Cross. Then – ha ha! – we'll do the chloroform stunt, Mr. McGonigle; cut you open, dive into your poor old guts, slosh around among your bowels for the bullet and then – ha! ha! ha! – sew you up again."

McGonigle, whose eyes were fixed on the ceiling, said feebly, "Doc, you better have another drink before you go. Have one yourself, Jimmy. This will be the last time I shall ever set 'em up to anybody on this earth. I'll have one, too, Jimmy."

Two days later word arrived at Midnapore that Peter J. had breathed his last on the operating table. The operation itself was declared to have been entirely successful, but it seems that Mr. McGonigle's heart, storm beaten as it was by many a howling gale of booze, had failed to rise to the occasion when the supreme call was made upon it.

Thus passed away a great spirit. The body was shipped back to Midnapore and interred in the little garden back of the printing office. The defunct Midnapore *Gazette* gave comfort, pleasure and instruction to many in its day, its contents being always an edifying and uplifting nature. McGonigle now belongs to history and the *Gazette* is a thing of the past.

Beware of spurious imitations.

The Ford is my jitney:
I shall not want for whiskey:
It maketh me to lie down in wet waters:
It soileth my clothes:
It leadeth me into deep waters:
It leadeth me into paths of ridicule
    for its namesake:
It prepareth a breakdown for me
    in the presence of mine enemies:
Yea, though I run through the valleys,
    I am towed up the hills.
I fear great evil when it is with me;
Its rods and its engines discomfort me.
It anointeth my face with oil.
Its tank runneth over.
Surely to goodness, if this thing follows me
    all the days of my life
      I shall dwell in the house of Ponoka forever.

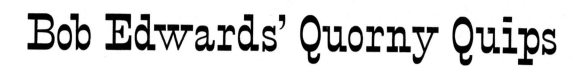

Bob Edwards' Quorny Quips

Dr. Gillespie met a ragged urchin one day in the streets of Glasgow, when the following conversation took place:

"Who looks after you, my laddie?"

"Naebuddy."

"Have you no father?"

"Faither's deid."

"And your mother?"

"No livin'."

"No sister."

"Naw."

"Any brothers?"

"Ay, yin."

"Well, can he not look after you! Where is he?"

"In Glesca College."

"How long has he been there?"

"Three years."

"Dear me, three years at the university, and can't help his little brother. What is he doing in the College?"

"Please, sir, he's in a bottle. He was born wi' two heids."

"Well, my little man," said the kindly old lady to a lonesome-looking kid," and who is your father?"

"Ain't got none."

"Poor boy! And who is your mother?"

"Never had any."

"Bless my soul, who are you anyhow?"

"I'm a mean trick that was played on auntie."

※

Jones observed an old lady sitting across the room.

"For heaven's sake!" he remarked to Robinson, "who is that extraordinarily ugly woman there?"

"That," answered Robinson, "is my wife."

Jones was taken aback, but moved up front again.

"Well," he said persuasively, "you just ought to see mine!"

A young man, an only son, married against his parents' wishes. Afterward, in telling a friend how to break the news to them, he said:

"Start off by telling them that I am dead, and then gently work up to the climax."

※

"Can you give me a recipe for making rice pudding?" – *Minnie.*

Answer. No we can't.

"Can you tell me how to get rid of vermin?" – *Esmeralda.*

Answer. No.

"What is the population of Pekin?" – *Student.*

Answer. Haven't the faintest idea.

"Could you – do you think you could marry a man like me?"

"Why, yes. That is, if he wasn't too much like you."

※

A well-known physician was examining a class of nurses. He described the condition of a patient, and asked one nurse how much morphine, in her opinion, should be administered to the sufferer.

"Eight grains," promptly replied the nurse.

The doctor made no comment, and the girl passed on. When her turn came again she appeared greatly confused, and said to the examiner.

"Doctor, I wish to correct the answer I made last time. I meant to say that one-eighth of a grain should be given to the patient."

"Too late," remarked the physician without looking up from his question paper. "The man's dead."

Bob Edwards wrote this caption in his Summer Annual: "Portrait of a poor chap who tried to keep tabs on the laws of his country, Dominion, Provincial and Civil. He is now an inmate of the Lunatic Asylum."

The way Edwards saw it, Canada's "War Lord" Sir Sam H. wasn't alone in his high opinion of himself. Another sketch of the World War I Minister was captioned: "Sam Hughes commanding the sun to stand still."

A PRAYER by Bob Edwards

O almighty dollar, without thee in the world we can do nothing; but with thee we can do all things. Be with us, we pray thee, in all thy decimal parts, for thou are the only one altogether lovely, and the chief among ten thousand. We feel that there is no condition in life where thy potent and all-powerful charms are not felt. In thy absence how gloomy is the household, and how desolate the hearthstone; but, in thy presence, how gleefully the beefsteak sings on the gridiron, how genial is the warmth that anthracite coal or tamarack wood diffuses throughout the apartment, and with an exuberance of joy continues to swell every bosom; thou are the joy of our youth and the solace of old age. Thou canst adorn the gentleman and feed the jackass; thou art the favorite of the philosopher, and the ideal of the lunkheads when an election is to be carried. Almighty dollar, thy shining face bespeaks thy wondrous power. In my pocket make thy resting place; I need thee every hour. And now, almighty dollar, in closing this invocation, we realize and acknowledge that thou art the god of our grand-fathers, the twofold god of their children, and the threefold god of their grand-children. Permit us to possess thee in abundance, is our constant and unwavering prayer.

Amen.

In a dull Scottish village, on a dull morning, one neighbor called at another's house. He was met at the door by his friend's wife.

"Cauld?"

"Ay."

"Is John in?"

"Och, ay! he's in."

"Can I see him?"

"Na."

"But a wanted tae see him."

"Ay, but you canna see him. John's dead."

"Deid?"

"Ay."

"Sudden?"

"Ay."

"Verra sudden?"

"Ay, verra sudden."

"Did he say onything aboot a pot o' green paint afore he deid?"

At the beginning of the 1900s, there was hardly a man or boy in Canada who couldn't recite, with dramatic quaverings of voice, at least the first few lines of a poem that began:

> A bunch of the boys were whooping it up
> In the Malamute Saloon
> The kid that handles the music box
> Was hitting a jagtime tune

It was written by a mild-mannered Scot named Robert W. Service who, during the aftermath of the Klondike gold rush was working as a bank clerk in Whitehorse, Yukon, writing poems and sticking them in his desk drawer. No one was interested in publishing them. Finally, Service paid to have them published himself. It was a rare and spectacular case of what's now known as "vanity" publishing paying off. His first book, *Songs of a Sourdough,* sold about one million copies. Service became the most frequently recited, best known popular poet in Canada. He made a fortune, went to France to live and spent 28 years there, much of the time on the Riviera. He became a health faddist and wrote a book called *Why Not Grow Young?* He also wrote 30 humorous songs, only one of which was successful. But people still remember, and, when the beer is flowing, recite, half seriously, half in fun, his epics of the Canadian Northwest.

The Ballad of Blasphemous Bill

Robert W. Service

I took a contract to bury the body of blasphemous
    Bill MacKie,
Whenever, wherever or whatsoever the manner of
    death he die –
Whether he die in the light o' day or under the
    peak-faced moon;
In cabin or dance-hall, camp or dive, mucklucks
    or patent shoon;
On velvet tundra or virgin peak, by glacier, drift
    or draw;
In muskeg hollow or canyon gloom, by avalanche,
    fang or claw;
By battle, murder or sudden wealth, by pestilence,
    hooch or lead –
I swore on the Book I would follow and look till I
    found my tombless dead.
For Bill was a dainty kind of cuss, and his mind
    was mighty sot
On a dinky patch with flowers and grass in a civilized
    bone-yard lot.
And where he died or how he died, it didn't matter
    a damn
So long as he had a grave with frills and a tombstone
    "epigram."
So I promised him, and he paid the price in good
    cheechako coin
(Which the same I blowed in that very night down
    in the Tenderloin.)
Then I painted a three-foot slab of pine: "Here
    lies poor Bill MacKie,"
And I hung it up on my cabin wall and I waited
    for Bill to die.
Years passed away, and at last one day came a
    squaw with a story strange,
Of a long-deserted line of traps 'way back of the
    Bighorn range;
Of a little hut by the great divide, and a white man
    stiff and still,
Lying there by his lonesome self, and I figured it
    must be Bill.
So I thought of the contract I'd made with him,
    and I took down from the shelf
The swell black box with the silver plate he'd picked
    out for hisself;

And I packed it full of grub and "hootch," and I
    slung it on the sleigh;
Then I harnessed up my team of dogs and was off
    at dawn of day.
You know what it's like in the Yukon wild when
    it's sixty-nine below;
When the ice-worms wriggle their purple heads
    through the crust of the pale blue snow;
When the pine-trees crack like little guns in the
    silence of the wood,
And the icicles hang down like tusks under the
    parka hood;
When the stove-pipe smoke breaks sudden off, and
    the sky is weirdly lit,
And the careless feel of a bit of steel burns like a
    red-hot spit;
When the mercury is a frozen ball, and the frost-fiend
    stalks to kill –
Well, it was just like that that day when I set out
    to look for Bill.
Oh, the awful hush that seemed to crush me down
    on every hand,
As I blundered blind with a trail to find through
    that blank and bitter land;
Half dazed, half crazed in the winter wild, with its
    grim heart-breaking woes,
And the ruthless strife for a grip on life that only
    the sourdough knows!
North by the compass, North I pressed; river and
    peak and plain
Passed like a dream I slept to lose and I waked to
    dream again.
River and plain and mighty peak – and who could
    stand unawed?
As their summits blazed, he could stand undazed
    at the foot of the throne of God.
North, aye, North, through a land accurst, shunned
    by the scouring brutes,
And all I heard was my own harsh word and the
    whine of the malemutes,
Till at last I came to a cabin squat, built in the side
    of a hill,
And I burst in the door, and there on the floor,
    frozen to death, lay Bill.
Ice, white ice, like a winding-sheet, sheathing each
    smoke-grimed wall;
Ice on the stove-pipe, ice on the bed, ice gleaming
    over all;
Sparkling ice on the dead man's chest, glittering
    ice in his hair,
Ice on his fingers, ice in his heart, ice in his glassy
    stare;

Hard as a log and trussed like a frog, with his arms
    and legs outspread.
I gazed at the coffin I'd brought for him, and I
    gazed at the gruesome dead,
And at last I spoke: "Bill like his joke; but still,
    goldarn his eyes,
A man had ought to consider his mates in the way
    he goes and dies."
Have you ever stood in an Arctic hut in the shadow
    of the Pole,
With a little coffin six by three and a grief you
    can't control?
Have you ever sat by a frozen corpse that looks
    at you with a grin,
And that seems to say: "You may try all day, but
    you'll never jam me in?"
I'm not a man of the quitting kind, but I never
    felt so blue
As I sat there gazing at that stiff and studying
    what I'd do.
Then I rose and I kicked off the husky dogs that
    were nosing round about,
And I lit a roaring fire in the stove, and I started
    to thaw Bill out.
Well, I thawed and thawed for thirteen days, but
    it didn't seem no good;
His arms and legs stuck out like pegs, as if they
    was made of wood.
Till at last I said: "It ain't no use – he's froze too
    hard to thaw;
He's obstinate, and he won't lie straight, so I guess
    I got to – saw."
So I sawed off poor Bill's arms and legs, and I laid
    him snug and straight
In the little coffin he picked hisself, with the dinky
    silver plate;
And I came nigh near to shedding a tear as I nailed
    him safely down;
Then I stowed him away in my Yukon sleigh, and
    I started back to town.
So I buried him as the contract was in a narrow
    grave and deep,
And there he's waiting the Great Clean-up, when
    The Judgment sluice-heads sweep;
And I smoke my pipe and I meditate in the light of
    the Midnight Sun,
And sometimes I wonder if they *was*, the awful
    things I done.
And as I sit and the parson talks, expounding of
    the Law,
I often think of poor old Bill – *and how hard he was
    to saw.*

THE

POLITICAL

SCENE

OLITICIAN DRAWINGS BY PETER WHALLEY

At length, he heard a council meeting was being held, and thither the colonel repaired. A man of his fine presence and military bearing was not to be put off by the man on guard at the door, and John A. was called out – and came.

"God bless my soul, Colonel Playfair, is that you!" exclaimed Sir John, grasping him with both hands. "How are you? I'm so glad to see you. By-the-bye, Colonel," he went on, after the greetings were over, "we have just been discussing in council a military matter that we cannot decide. Now you, with your great military experience and your memories of Salamanca and Talavera will be able to solve the question."

The colonel drew himself up and looked grave.

"The question is," said John A., "how many pounds of powder put under a bull's tail would blow his horns off?"

And John A., who had been edging toward his office, disappeared through the door and could be seen no more.*

– Anecdodal Life of Sir John Macdonald,
E. B. Biggar

The picture of Canada's parliament, beginning with the famous one of the Fathers of Confederation, consisting of sombre men looking to the future, heads full of human destiny, is a handy convention but not necessarily true. Canada's politicians have exhibited a sense of humour ranging from sharp wit to low burlesque. Sometimes political behaviour has verged on wild slapstick. An amazing example is the great debate of 1878, which might be called "The Night the Canadian Government Cracked Up," reported by E. B. Biggar.

The all-night debate

The great all-night debate, with which the session of the spring of 1878 closed, had no parallel before or since the Government was established at Ottawa. While points of order were being argued, members hammered at desks, blew on tin trumpets, imitated the crowing of cocks, sent up toy balloons, threw sand-crackers of torpedoes, and occasionally hurled blue books across the House. Often the babel of sounds was such that neither the Speaker of the House nor the member who had the floor could be heard. Once in a while amid the din some member with a good voice would start up the *Marsellaise, God Save the Queen, A la claire fontaine, The Raftsman's chorus,* or some plantation melody, and then the whole House would join in the song, with an effect that was quite moving. The feelings inspired by these songs would sway the House back into a quiet frame; but scarcely would the speaker who had the floor recover the thread of his discourse when such a pandemonium would be raised as made the listener think "Chaos has come again." When a speaker had at last made himself heard over the diminishing din of exhausted voices, and when he himself had exhausted his subject, he would keep the floor by quoting passages from law-books, books of poetry, philosophy and humour.

Mr. Cimon, one of these speakers, filled up his time by reading the whole of the British North America Act in French, making humorous comments upon each clause. In some of these passages "the grim features of Mr. Blake," writes a chronicler of the scene, "not merely relaxed into a smile, but broke into a laugh, that shook his big frame all over."

As the night wore on, the spectators became tired, and the galleries were gradually cleared. Now and again a member strayed off, and would be found shortly afterwards stretched on a bench in the reading-room, or curled up in an alcove of the library fast asleep. But there were always enough members left in the House to keep up the fun. Even here, however, the exhausted figures of some members would be found reclining on their desks, quite unconscious of the paper missiles that were being pelted at them. In the afternoon Lady Dufferin had sat in the gallery, listening with amused bewilderment to the babel of sounds. As she rose to leave, a member struck up *God Save the Queen,* and all the House rose and joined in the anthem with a patriotic fervor that was remarkable. Mr. Mackenzie had just come in at that moment, and Mr. Blake and he, after looking at each other in hesitation for a few moments, threw off their dignity and joined in. Just as the singing ceased, Sir John, who had been resting in his private room, appeared on the scene, and was greeted with a rousing cheer by the Opposition.

At one stage Mr. De Veber rose to a point of order. The Speaker asked what it was, and De Veber said, "The Minister of Marine and Fisheries is sitting at the clerk's table in irreverent proximity to the mace."

"That's no point of order," said the Speaker, and

30

*In fairness to Canada's first prime minister, he was just having a joke. He had already approved the colonel's appointment.

πολυμητις Οδυσσευς

Sir John A. Macdonald

in the midst of the laughter which followed some one struck up *Auld Lang Syne.*

A party of members organized an impromptu band, which was nicknamed "Gideon's Band," and began to play a species of music that was more discordant if possible than the voices and banging of desks which accompanied it. Mr. Cheval, a French member, had procured some new instruments described as "squeaking machines," and these were added to the band. Some one wanted to put down Mr. Cheval and his music, upon which he pathetically appealed to the Speaker. "Mr. Speaker, I wish to know which is more worse, de man dat trows blue books 'cross de House, or de man dat goes in for a small leedle music." This entreaty was received with roars of laughter. The Speaker said both were unparliamentary, whereupon Mr. Smith of Peel, whose role was leader of the orchestra, led off the House in another song, while Mr. Cheval resumed operations on his squeaking machine. Mr. Blake kept himself amused and awake "by performing some extraordinary finger-music on his desk." Mr. Smith of Peel got so hoarse from his orchestral performances that he simply croaked.

At one point in the proceedings Mr. Campbell, horrified at this outrage upon decorum, came out near the clerk's table, and with the most violent gesticulations, swinging his arms and waving his hat, denounced the proceedings. Mr. Mackenzie demanded that the Sergeant-at-arms should be called in to preserve order, but the Sergeant-at-arms, esconced in a private nook of his own, was enjoying the fun too much to do anything of the kind.

While this had been going on Lady Dufferin again came in, and when she left, the House once more gave *God Save the Queen,* followed up with a cheer and such waving of handkerchiefs as would have led a stranger to believe that Queen Victoria herself was quitting the Chamber.

At last Mr. Cheval burst his toy bag-pipe and retired with a broken heart, amid the mock sympathy of his orchestra. A demand by Mr. Dymond for a speech from the Speaker was greeted with roars of laughter. At 4.15 a.m., that patient functionary left Mr. De Veber in his chair and went out to get something to eat. In a few moments pages began to bring in coffee, which was greeted with cheers from both sides. About six o'clock (at which hour, had it been evening, the Speaker would have risen from the chair as a matter of course), Mr. Bowell rose and said he was willing to have six o'clock called, and go on after getting something to eat.

"There is no six o'clock to-day," added Mr. Holton.

"Six o'clock was yesterday," added Mr. Mills.

"Oh, it's six of one and half a dozen of the other," said Mr. Blake.

"Then it's twelve," reasoned Mr. Bowell, amid laughter.

The House finally adjourned, after sitting for twenty-seven hours!

BENNETT

An English tourist in Canada was being shown the sights of Ottawa by a professional guide. The Englishman finally asked, "Who is that old man walking round and round Parliament House muttering to himself?"

The guide replied after a glance, "Oh! that is Mr. Bennett, sir, Prime Minister of the Dominion. He is holding a meeting of the cabinet."

– Throop's Scrapbook

KING

Mr. Esling: My references were to the religious fanatics who today are offending the public by exhibitions of absolute nakedness. In order to bring this right home I would like to know what the Prime Minister would think if he went into his garden in the morning to pick pansies or violets and was confronted by six naked Doukhobors.

Mr. King: I would send for my honorable friend the Leader of the Opposition and the leader of the Progressive Party.

Mr. Bennett: There would be a riot if you overlooked your own supporters.

– House of Commons, 1928

DIEFENBAKER

Rt. Hon. J. G. Diefenbaker: I think many people now realize as never before that this Government is inadequate, inept, indecisive . . .

Mr. MacEachern: And in office.

– *House of Commons,* 1966

HEPBURN

Mitchell Hepburn (at an Ontario political meeting where a manure spreader was used as a platform): This is the first time I've ever been on a Tory platform.

Tory voice: Throw her into high, Mitch, she's got the biggest load now she'll ever have.

– *Throop's Scrapbook*

While Duncan Ross was speaking in the Ontario Legislature, a Conservative member, bantering, called out "Order." Mr. Speaker was asleep but suddenly woke up and solemnly said, "The Member for West Middlesex is out of order."

"In what respect," asked Mr. Ross.

The Speaker responded, "I don't know, but if you'll kindly repeat what you were saying, I'll let you know."

– *More Candid Chronicles*

Hon. W. R. Motherwell: C.C.F. friends over there are all full of an abundance of hot air and heifer dust.

– *House of Commons,* 1934

BROWN

I know enough of the feelings of this meeting to know you would rather have John A. drunk than George Brown sober.

– *Sir John A. Macdonald*

In the western islands of Scotland, in the days of old, the wreck of a ship was considered a better crop than the usual crop of oats, and they used to pray sometimes for a good season and plenty of wrecks. It is said that on one occasion, on a Sunday while a clergyman was giving a good Calvinistic sermon, a person rushed into the church and evident uneasiness came over the congregation. The parson twigged at once that there was a ship in distress in the offing, so, he said, "My friends, keep your seats. Listen to the words of wisdom; do not be carried away by feelings of love for filthy lucre" . . . Unbuttoning the door of the pulpit, and making a dash for the door, he added . . . "But let us have a fair start at all events."

– *Sir John A. Macdonald,*
House of Commons, 1894

At a small country schoolhouse, Dr. Michael Clark was annoyed by an opponent who kept shouting, "Louder." Clark's rejoinder was: "Ladies and gentlemen, the Bible tells us that the Heavens shall vanish away like smoke and the earth wax old like a garment, and they that dwell therein shall be in like manner. And on that day Gabriel will sound his horn, and the righteous will be gathered up into Heaven and the wicked cast into outer darkness. And I have no doubt at all, friends, that when that day comes, and the trumpet sounds, my diminutive friends back of the stove will shout 'Louder'."

– *Dr. Michael Clark*, by Dr. G. D. Stanley

33

PERSONALITIES BY LA PALME

W. L. MACKENZIE KING

LOUIS ST. LAURENT

EARL ALEXANDER   (OPENING THE MONTREAL PRESS CLUB)

Robert LaPalme, French Canada's famed cartoonist, deftly spears the high and mighty on the point of his pen.

I cannot but remember the story of the Jew going into an eating house and being seduced by a slice of ham. When he came out it so happened that there was a crash of thunder and he said: "Good heavens, what a row about a little bit of pork."

– *Sir John A. Macdonald*

Long after being elected Canada's first woman member of parliament, Agnes Macphail said: "If I had known what it meant for a woman to invade a man's world, I wouldn't have been able to face it." **But,** having established, and held, the beachhead, she never stopped needling men.

If there are a few chickens, a woman looks after them: if there's a well-paying flock of 5,000 a man takes over. If it's baking a few pies, a woman does it; if it becomes Mother Somebody-or-Other's Home-made Pastry with coast-to-coast distribution, the boys get together and organize it.

Men act like selfish children. They are spoiled from the time they are born, first by their mothers, then by their wives and daughters. If a man loses a collar button he simply needs to make a noise and his wife or his daughters find it for him. My own father was a dear fellow, but I don't think he ever in his life found his shirt and his studs at the same time. He could usually find his shirt and sometimes he could find his studs, but never did he find both his shirt and his studs at once.

The world is full of "grand old men" who could go on a two-year cruise without being missed as long as their secretaries are on the job to look after things. Why are there no "grand old women?"

Why is a fumbling male human known as an "old woman?" He isn't an old woman, or anything like an old woman. If he were an old woman he'd have some sense. What he is is a fuddle-headed old man. Why not say so?

When men are backed up by one another their morale is at its usual high. But one man in an audience is a problem. You can't call a spade a spade. You must be constantly reminding yourself that a bundle of sensitivity and puffed ego is present. It's a terrible bore to women who are trying to get things done.

Maclean's, 1949

Heckler, during speech by Agnes Macphail, M.P.: "Don't you wish you were a man?"
Miss Macphail: "Yes. Don't you?"

STEPHEN LEACOCK

a selection from Canada's greatest humorist

Just before World War I, Canadians began to laugh over the essays of a man who was to become the most widely read, durable and all-round-successful humorist Canada has produced – Stephen Leacock, the professor who wrote humour as a sideline while teaching political economy at McGill University. Leacock followed Mark Twain as the No. 1 ranking humorist in America. For over 50 years he has been anthologized, reprinted, quoted, imitated, translated and eulogized, and he deserves every bit of it. His material is as fresh and entertaining today as it ever was. Nobody has topped him and few have come near him. I found that one of the toughest jobs in keeping to the space limitations of this book was deciding what pieces of Leacock's to use and what to leave out. I'd no sooner put something in than I'd decide that something else was even funnier, and take it out. I included *Lord Oxhead's Secret*, from his *Nonsense Novels,* and *The Yahi-Bahi Oriental Society of Mrs. Rasselyer-Brown*, from *Arcadian Adventures with the Idle Rich,* then took them out, then read them over again and tried to find room to put them in again.

I must have changed the selections half a dozen times. I still have complete Leacock stories typed out, wishing I could find room for them.

It's hard to say exactly why Leacock was so good, but if I had to try I'd say one of the main things was that he never merely tried to be funny; he saw the fun in situations, which is an entirely different thing. There isn't a "funny" word or description in his *Boarding-House Geometry*. Yet I've never been able to read it aloud to friends without my voice quavering, and usually I begin sputtering so much I spoil the reading. The piece is funny because Leacock's feeling about boarding-houses is funny. So is his attitude to Russian novels and Greek epic poetry. There's hardly any visible effort to be funny in either *Sorrows of a Super Soul* or *Homer and Humbug*, yet his overall attitude to these commentaries on High Art makes them among the funniest things ever written.

Another thing, Leacock was full of fun, which also is drastically different than trying to be funny. I started to laugh at Leacock myself when, in my teens, I read his newspaper account of a lecture tour he made out West. Leacock described the way the reporters on his route introduced him to their readers, starting in Toronto by depicting him as a quiet, medium-sized, modest, rather indistinguished looking man, and, making him smaller, more modest and more undistinguished the further he went west, until, in Vancouver, I think it was, they wrote: "The train stopped and a trembling, timid little mouse of a man crawled out from under his golf bag."

It's always been hard for me to realize that he was a professor. He belonged on the other side of the lecture platform. There was nothing academic about his humour. He simply took off every now and then in flights of high literary spirits, as he did in his frenzied ode to a dentist in *The Perfect Optimist*. That kind of humour is disastrous if it misses. Leacock was almost always bang-on, because the feeling of fun was there. The only book of his I've never been able to get into was the one for which he was most famous – *Sunshine Sketches of a Little Town*, a satire on small-town life. It's the only one in which, to me, he seems to be self-consciously clever and patronizing.

There's amazingly little biographical material about Leacock. He was born on the Isle of Wight in 1869. "I am not aware that there was any particular conjunction of the planets at the time," he wrote in a preface to *Sunshine Sketches*. "My parents migrated to Canada in 1876, and I decided to go with them. My father took up a farm near Lake Simcoe, in Ontario. I saw enough of farming to speak exuberantly in political addresses of the joy of early rising and

The Rev. Mr. Drone, of Mariposa, takes his daily post-prandial nap. He is in the cast of Stephen Leacock's Sunshine Sketches of a Little Town.

the deep sleep, both of body and intellect, that is induced by honest manual toil." (Later, when he was a successful writer, operating his farm as a hobby, he reported in a letter to his niece Barbara Nimmo, "Ten years ago the deficit on my farm was about a hundred dollars; but by well designed capital expenditure, by drainage and by greater attention to details, I have got it into the thousands.")

He went to Upper Canada College and the University of Toronto, and after graduation returned to Upper Canada College as housemaster, a job he described as "the most dreary, the most thankless, and the worst paid profession in the world." While there he began writing the short humour pieces for magazines and newspapers which were to appear in book form in 1910 under the title of *Literary Lapses*. After teaching for eight years, he took his doctor of philosophy degree at the University of Chicago, and was appointed lecturer at McGill in 1901. He was made head of the Department of Economics and Political Science in 1908.

Reminiscing about his doctorate, he wrote, "The meaning of this degree is that the recipient of instruction is examined for the last time in his life, and is pronounced completely full. After this, no new ideas can be imparted to him."

Leacock had his share of quirks. He disliked talking over radio, hated the telephone, never learned to drive, and kept elaborate financial accounts of his farm. "He nearly went on an expedition to the South Pole," wrote Barbara Nimmo, " – was it with Shackleton or Vilhjalmur Stefansson? I forget; he knew them both. But when he found he could not take along his own supply of whiskey, the long, cold nights of the Antarctic seemed too much."

Another niece, reminiscing about her uncle, said, "We children would all be enjoying ourselves in our own way, say, playing on our raft at Lake Simcoe, then Uncle Stephen would arrive and do the big hamper bit and say we were all going on a picnic to Uncle Charlie's bush. We didn't want to go, but we had to. We'd just get to the bush and start enjoying ourselves exploring when he'd push us all into the cars and tell us we were going some place else. He was an absolute tyrant."

Leacock was forced to retire from McGill in 1936, and in an essay *A Lecture on Walking*, he wrote, "It is now six years since an ungrateful college foiled me, on the mere ground of senile decline, to give any more lectures, and took away all my students."

It's a good thing for Canada, and the world, that the nonsensical idea of compulsory retirement wasn't able to take Stephen Leacock away from his readers.

The Perfect Optimist
or
Daydreams in a dental chair

Well, here we are again seated in the big red plush chair in for one of our jolly little mornings with our dentist. My! It certainly is cosy to settle back into this comfortable chair with a whole quiet morning in front of us – no work to do, no business to think of, just to lie in one of our comfortable daydreams.

How pleasant it is in this chair, anyway, with the sunshine streaming in through the window upon us and illuminating every corner of the neat and immaculate little room in which we sit.

For immaculate neatness and cleanliness, I repeat, give me a little up-to-date dental room every time. Talk of your cosy libraries or your dens, they won't compare with this little nook. Here we are with everything we need around us, all within easy arm's-length reach. Here on this revolving tray are our pleasant little nippers, pincers and forceps, some so small and cute and others so big and strong that we feel a real confidence in them. They'd never let go of anything! Here is our dainty little electric buzzer with our revolving gimlets at the end; our little hammer on the left; our bradawl on the right – everything!

For the moment our dental friend is out of the room – telephoning, we imagine. The merry fellow is so popular with all his friends that they seem to ring him up every few minutes.

Little scraps of his conversation reach our ears as we lie half-buried in our white towel, in a sweet reverie of expectancy.

'Pretty bad in the night, was it, eh? Well, perhaps you'd better come along down and we'll make a boring through that bicuspid and see what's there!'

Full of ideas, he is, always like that – never discouraged, something new to suggest all the time. And then we hear him say: 'Well, let me see. I'm busy now for about a couple of hours . . .' Hurrah! That means us! We were so afraid he was going to say, 'I'll be through here in about five minutes.' But now it's all right; we've got two long, dreamy hours in front of us.

He comes back into the room, and his cheery presence, as he searches among his instruments and gives a preliminary buzz to the buzzer, seems to make the sunshine even brighter. How pleasant life seems – the dear old life; that is, the life we quitted ten minutes ago and to which, please Providence, we hope to return in two hours. We never felt till we sat here how full and pleasant life is. Think of it, the simple joy of being alive. That's all we ask – of going to work each day (without a toothache) and coming home each night to eat our dinner. If only people realized it – just to live in our world without a toothache . . .

So runs our pleasant reverie. But, meanwhile, our dental friend has taken up a little hammer and has tapped us, in his playful way, on the back teeth.

'Feel that?' he asks.

And he's right, the merry dog! We *do* feel it. He guessed it right away. We are hoping so much that he will hit us again.

Come on, let's have a little more fun like that. But no. He's laid aside his hammer and as nearly as we can see has rolled up his cuffs to the elbow and has started his good old electric buzzer into a roar.

Ah, ha! Now we are going to get something – this is going to be the big fun, the real thing. That's the greatest thing about our little dental mornings, there's always something new. Always as we sit we have a pleasant expectancy that our dental friend is planning a new one.

Now, then, let us sit back tight, while he drives at our jaw with the buzzer. Of all the exhilarating feelings of hand-to-hand conflict, of man against man, of mind matched against mind, and intelligence pitted against intelligence, I know of none more stimulating than when we brace ourselves for this conflict of man and machinery. He has on his side the power of electricity and the force of machinery.

But we are not without resource. We brace ourselves, laughingly, in our chair while he starts to bore. We need, in fact, our full strength; but, on the other hand, if he tries to keep up at this pace his hands will get tired. We realize, with a sense of amusement, that if his machine slips, he may get a nasty thump on the hand against our jawbone.

He slacks off for just a second, half withdraws his machine and says, 'Were you at the football match yesterday?' and then starts his instrument again at full roar.

'Were we at the football match yesterday?' How strange it sounds! 'Why, yes, of course we were!' In

that far-away long-ago world where they play football and where there is no toothache – we were there only yesterday afternoon.

Yes, we remember, it was just towards the end of that game that we felt those twinges in one of the – what does he call it, the lower molars? Anyway, one of those twinges which started the exultant idea racing through our minds, 'To-morrow we'll have to go to the dentist.'

A female voice speaking into the room has called him to the telephone, and again we are alone. What if he never comes back!

The awful thought leaps to our minds, what if he comes in and says, 'I'm sorry to say I have to take a train out of town at once.' How terrible!

Perhaps he'll come in and say, 'Excuse me, I have to let your work go; they've sent for me to go to China!'

But no, how lucky! Back he comes again. We've not lost him. And now what is he at? Stuffing cotton-wool up into our head, wool saturated with some kind of drugs, and pounding it in with a little hammer.

And then – all of a sudden, so it seems – he steps back and says, 'There, that will do nicely till Monday!' And we rise half-dazed from our chair to realize in our disappointment that it is over already. Somehow we had thought that our pleasant drowsy morning of pounding and boring and dreaming in the sunlight, while our dental friend mixed up something new, would last for ever. And now, all of a sudden, it is over.

Never mind! After all, he said Monday! It won't seem so long till then! And meantime we can think about it all day and look forward to it and imagine how it is going to feel. Oh! It won't be long.

And so we step out into the street – full of cotton-wool and drugs and electricity and reverie – like a person returning to a forgotten world and dazed to find it there.

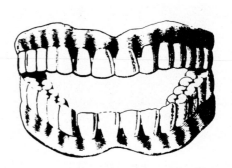

Boarding House Geometry

Axioms and definitions

All boarding-houses are the same boarding-house.

Boarders in the same boarding-house and on the same flat are equal to one another.

A single room is that which has no parts and no magnitude.

The landlady of a boarding-house is a parallelogram – that is, an oblong angular figure, which cannot be described, but which is equal to anything.

A wrangle is the disinclination for each other of two boarders that meet together but are not in the same line.

All the other rooms being taken, a single room is said to be a double room.

Postulates and Propositions

A pie may be produced any number of times.

The landlady can be reduced to her lowest terms by a series of propositions.

A bee line may be made from any boarding-house to any other boarding-house.

The clothes of a boarding-house bed, though produced ever so far both ways, will not meet.

Any two meals at a boarding-house are together less than two square meals.

If from the opposite ends of a boarding-house a line be drawn passing through all rooms in turn, then the stovepipe which warms the boarders will lie within that line.

On the same bill and on the same side of it there should not be two charges for the same thing.

If there be two boarders on the same flat, and the amount of side of the one be equal to the amount of side of the other, each to each, and the wrangle between one boarder and the landlady be equal to the wrangle between the landlady and the other, then shall the weekly bills of the two boarders be equal also, each to each.

For if not, let one bill be the greater.

Then the other bill is less than it might have been – which is absurd.

Roughing it in the bush

My plans for moose hunting in the Canadian wilderness

The season is now opening when all those who have a manly streak in them like to get out into the bush and rough it for a week or two of hunting or fishing. For myself, I never feel that the autumn has been well spent unless I can get out after the moose. And, when I go, I like to go right into the bush and 'rough it' – get clear away from civilization, out in the open, and take fatigue and hardship just as it comes.

So this year I am making all my plans to get away for a couple of weeks of moose-hunting along with my brother George and my friend Tom Gass. We generally go together because we are all of us men who like the rough stuff, and are tough enough to stand the hardship of living in the open. The place we go to is right in the heart of the primitive Canadian forest, among big timber, broken with lakes as still as glass, just the very ground for moose.

We have a kind of lodge up there. It's just a rough place that we put up, the three of us, the year before last – built out of tamarack logs faced with a broad axe. The flies, while we were building it, were something awful. Two of the men that we sent in there to build it were so badly bitten that we had to bring them out a hundred miles to a hospital. None of us saw the place while we were building it – we were all busy at the time – but the teamsters who took in our stuff said it was the worst season for the black flies that they ever remembered.

Still we hung on to it, in spite of the flies, and stuck at it till we got it built. It is, as I say, only a plain place, but good enough to rough it in. We have one big room with a stone fireplace, and bedrooms round the sides, with a wide veranda, properly screened, all along the front. The veranda has a row of upright tamaracks for its posts, and doesn't look altogether bad. In the back part we have quarters where our man sleeps. We had an ice-house knocked up while they were building, and water laid on in pipes from a stream. So that, on the whole, the place has a kind of rough comfort about it – good enough, anyway, for fellows hunting moose all day.

The place, nowadays, is not hard to get at. The Government has just built a colonization highway, quite all right for motors, that happens to go within a hundred yards of our lodge.

We can get the railway for a hundred miles, and then the highway for forty, and the last hundred yards we can walk. But this season we are going to cut out the railway and go the whole way from the city in George's car, with our kit with us.

George has one of those great big cars with a roof and thick glass sides. Personally, none of the three of us would have preferred to ride in a luxurious darned thing like that. Tom says that, as far as he is concerned, he'd much sooner go into the bush over a rough trail in a buckboard; and, for my own part, a team of oxen would be more the kind of thing I'd wish.

However, the car is there, so we might as well use the thing, especially as the provincial Government has built the fool highway right into the wilderness. By taking the big car also we can not only carry all the hunting outfit that we need, but we can also, if we like, shove in a couple of small trunks with a few clothes. This may be necessary, as it seems that somebody has gone and slapped a great big frame hotel right there in the wilderness, not half a mile from the place we go to. The hotel we find a regular nuisance. It gave us the advantage of electric light for our lodge (a thing none of us cares about), but it means more fuss about clothes. Clothes, of course, don't really matter when a fellow is roughing it in the bush, but Tom says that we might find it necessary to go over to the hotel in the evenings to borrow coal-oil or a side of bacon or any rough stuff that we need; and they do such a lot of dressing up at these fool hotels now, that if we do go over for bacon or anything in the evening we might just as well slip on our evening clothes, as we could chuck them off the minute we get back. George thinks it might not be a bad idea – just as a way of saving all our energy for getting after the moose – to dine each evening at the hotel itself. He knew some men who did that last year, and they told him that the time saved for moose-hunting in that way is extraordinary. George's idea is that we could come in each night with our moose – such-and-such a number as the case might be – either bringing them with us or burying them where they die, change our things, slide over to the hotel and get dinner, and then beat it back into the bush by moonlight and fetch in the moose. It seems

they have a regular two-dollar table d'hôte dinner at the hotel – just rough stuff of course, but after all, as we all admit, we don't propose to go out into the wilds to pamper ourselves with high feeding; a plain hotel meal in a home-like style at two dollars a plate is better than cooking up a lot of rich stuff over a camp-fire.

If we *do* dine at the hotel we could take our choice each evening between going back into the bush by moonlight to fetch in the dead moose from the different caches where we had hidden them, or sticking round the hotel itself for a while. It seems that there is dancing there. Nowadays such a lot of women and girls get the open-air craze for the life in the bush that these big wilderness hotels are crowded with them. There is something about living in the open that attracts modern women, and they like to get right away from everybody and everything; and, of course, hotels of this type in the open are nowadays always well closed in with screens so that there are no flies or anything of that sort.

So it seems that there is dancing at the hotel every evening, nothing on a large scale or pretentious, just an ordinary hardwood floor – they may wax it a little for all I know – and some sort of plain, rough Italian orchestra that they fetch up from the city. Not that any of us care for dancing. It's a thing that, personally, we wouldn't bother with. But it happens that there are a couple of young girls that Tom knows that are going to be staying at the hotel, and, of course, naturally he wants to give them a good time. They are only eighteen and twenty (sisters), and that's really younger than we care for, but with young girls like that – practically kids – any man wants to give them a good time. So Tom says, and I think quite rightly, that as the kids are going to be there we may as well put in an appearance at the hotel and see that they are having a good time. Their mother is going to be with them too, and of course we want to give her a good time as well; in fact, I think I will lend her my moose rifle and let her go out and shoot moose. One thing we are all agreed upon in the arrangement of our hunting trip is in not taking along anything to drink. Drinking spoils a trip of that sort. We all remember how in the old days we'd go out into a camp in the bush (I mean before there used to be any highway or any hotel), and carry in rye whisky in demi-johns (two dollars a gallon it was), and sit around the campfire drinking it in the evenings.

But there's nothing in it. We all agree that, the law being what it is, it is better to stick to it. It makes a fellow feel better. So we shall carry nothing in. I don't say that one might not have a flask of something in one's pocket in the car; but only as a precaution against accident or cold. And when we get to our lodge we all feel that we are a darned sight better without it. If we *should* need anything – though it isn't likely – there are still three cases of old Scotch whisky kicking around the lodge somewhere: I think they are kicking around in a little cement cellar with a locked door that we had made so as to use it for butter or anything of that sort. Anyway, there are three, possibly four, or maybe five, cases of Scotch there, and, if we should for any reason want it, there it is. But we are hardly likely to touch it – unless we hit a cold snap, or a wet spell; then we might; or if we strike hot, dry weather. Tom says he thinks there are a couple of cases of champagne still in the cellar – some stuff that one of us must have shot in there just before Prohibition came in. But we'll hardly use it. When a man is out moose-hunting from dawn to dusk he hasn't much use for champagne – not till he gets home, anyway. The only thing that Tom says the champagne might come in useful for would be if we cared to ask the two kids over to some sort of dinner; it would be just a rough kind of camp dinner (we could hardly ask their mother to it), but we think we could manage it. The man we keep there used to be a butler in England, or something of the sort, and he could manage some kind of rough meal where the champagne might fit in.

There's only one trouble about our plans for our fall camp that bothers us just a little. The moose are getting damn scarce about that place. There used, so they say, to be any quantity of them. There's an old settler up there that our man buys all our cream from, who says that he remembers when the moose were so thick that they would come up and drink whisky out of his dipper. But somehow they seem to have quit the place. Last year we sent our man out again and again looking for them, and he never saw any. Three years ago a boy that works at the hotel said he saw a moose in the cow pasture back of the hotel, and there were the tracks of a moose seen last year at the place not ten miles from the hotel where it had come to drink. But, apart from these two exceptions, the moose-hunting has been poor.

Still, what does it matter? What we want is the *life*, the rough life, just as I have described it. If any moose comes to our lodge, we'll shoot him, or tell the butler to. But if not – well, we've got along without for ten years. I don't suppose we shall worry.

How to live to be 200

Twenty years ago I knew a man called Jiggins, who had the Health Habit.

He used to take a cold plunge every morning. He said it opened his pores. After it he took a hot sponge. He said it closed the pores. He got so that he could open and shut his pores at will.

Jiggins used to stand and breathe at an open window for half an hour before dressing. He said it expanded his lungs. He might, of course, have had it done in a shoe-store with a boot stretcher, but after all it cost him nothing this way, and what is half an hour?

After he had got his undershirt on, Jiggins used to hitch himself up like a dog in harness and do Sandow exercises. He did them forwards, backwards, and hind-side up.

He could have got a job as a dog anywhere. He spent all his time at this kind of thing. In his spare time at the office, he used to lie on his stomach on the floor and see if he could lift himself up with his knuckles. If he could, then he tried some other way until he found one that he couldn't do. Then he would spend the rest of his lunch hour on his stomach, perfectly happy.

In the evenings in his room he used to lift iron bars, cannon-balls, heave dumb-bells, and haul himself up to the ceiling with his teeth. You could hear the thumps half a mile.

He liked it.

He spent half the night slinging himself around his room. He said it made his brain clear. When he got his brain perfectly clear, he went to bed and slept. As soon as he woke, he began clearing it again.

Jiggins is dead. He was, of course, a pioneer, but the fact that he dumb-belled himself to death at an early age does not prevent a whole generation of young men from following in his path.

They are ridden by the Health Mania.

They make themselves a nuisance.

They get up at impossible hours. They go out in silly suits and run Marathon heats before breakfast. They chase around barefoot to get the dew on their feet. They hunt for ozone. They bother about pepsin. They won't eat meat because it has too much nitrogen. They won't eat fruit because it hasn't any. They prefer albumen and starch and nitrogen to huckleberry pie and doughnuts. They won't drink water out of a tap. They won't eat sardines out of a can. They won't use oysters out of a pail. They won't drink milk out of a glass. They are afraid of alcohol in any shape. Yes, sir, afraid.

And after all their fuss they presently incur some simple old-fashioned illness and die like anybody else.

Now people of this sort have no chance to attain any great age. They are on the wrong track.

Listen. Do you want to live to be really old, to enjoy a grand, green, exuberant, boastful old age and to make yourself a nuisance to your whole neighbourhood with your reminiscences?

Then cut out all this nonsense. Cut it out. Get up in the morning at a sensible hour. The time to get up is when you have to, not before. If your office opens at eleven, get up at ten-thirty. Take your chance on ozone. There isn't any such thing anyway. Or, if there is, you can buy a Thermos bottle full for five cents, and put it on a shelf in your cupboard. If your work begins at seven in the morning, get up at ten minutes to, but don't be liar enough to say that you like it. It isn't exhilarating, and you know it.

Also, drop all that cold-bath business. You never did it when you were a boy. Don't be a fool now. If you must take a bath (you don't really need to), take it warm. The pleasure of getting out of a cold bed and creeping into a hot bath beats a cold plunge to death. In any case, stop gassing about your tub and your "shower," as if you were the only man who ever washed.

So much for that point.

Next, take the question of germs and bacilli. Don't be scared of them. That's all. That's the whole thing, and if you once get on to that you never need to worry again.

If you see a bacilli, walk right up to it, and look it in the eye. If one flies into your room, strike at it with your hat or with a towel. Hit it as hard as you can between the neck and the thorax. It will soon get sick of that.

But as a matter of fact, a bacilli is perfectly quiet and harmless if you are not afraid of it. Speak to it. Call out to it to "lie down." It will understand. I had a bacilli once, called Fido, that would come and lie at my feet while I was working. I never knew a more affectionate companion, and when it was run over by an automobile, I buried it in the garden with genuine sorrow.

(I admit this is an exaggeration. I don't really remember its name; it may have been Robert.)

Understand that it is only a fad of modern medicine to say that cholera and typhoid and diptheria are caused by baccili and germs; nonsense. Cholera is caused by a frightful pain in the stomach, and diphtheria is caused by trying to cure a sore throat.

Now take the question of food.

Eat what you want. Eat lots of it. Yes, eat too much of it. Eat till you can just stagger across the room with it and prop it up against a sofa cushion. Eat everything that you like until you can't eat any more. The only test is, can you pay for it? If you can't pay for it, don't eat it. And listen – don't worry as to whether your food contains starch, or albumen, or gluten, or nitrogen. If you are a damn fool enough to want these things, go and buy them and eat all you want of them. Go to a laundry and get a bag of starch, and eat your fill of it. Eat it, and take a good long drink of glue after it, and perhaps a heaping spoonful of Portland cement. That will gluten you, good and solid.

If you like nitrogen, go and get a druggist to give you a canful of it at the soda counter, and let you sip it with a straw. Only don't think that you can mix all these things up with your food. There isn't any nitrogen or phosphorus or albumen in ordinary things to eat. In any decent household all that sort of stuff is washed out in the kitchen sink before the food is put on the table.

And just one word about fresh air and exercise. Don't bother with either of them. Get your room full of good air, then shut up the windows and keep it. It will keep for years. Anyway, don't keep using your lungs all the time. Let them rest. As for exercise, if you have to take it, take it and put up with it. But as long as you have the price of a hack and can hire other people to play baseball for you and run races and do gymnastics when you sit in the shade and smoke and watch them – great heavens, what more do you want?

A clear view of the government and politics of England

A loyal British subject like myself in dealing with the government of England should necessarily begin with a discussion of the monarchy. I have never had the pleasure of meeting the King except once on the G.T.R. platform in Orillia, Ontario, when he was the Duke of York and I was one of the welcoming delegates of the Town Council. No doubt he would recall it in a minute.

But in England the King is surrounded by formality and circumstance. On many mornings I waited round the gates of Buckingham Palace but I found it quite impossible to meet the King in the quiet sociable way in which one met him in Orillia. The English, it seems, love to make the kingship a subject of great pomp and official etiquette. In Canada it is quite different. Perhaps we understand kings and princes better than the English do. At any rate we treat them in a far more human heart-to-heart fashion than is the English custom, and they respond to it at once.

I remember when King George – he was, as I say, Duke of York then – came up to Orillia, Ontario, how we all met him in a delegation on the platform. Bob Curran – Bob was Mayor of the town that year – went up to him and shook hands with him and invited him to come right on up to Orillia House where he had a room reserved for him. Charlie Janes and Mel Tudhope and the other boys who were on the Town Council gathered round the royal Prince and shook hands and told him that he simply must stay over. George Rapley, the bank manager, said that if he wanted a cheque cashed or anything of that sort to come right into the Royal Bank and he would do it for him. The Prince had two *aides-de-camp* with him and a secretary, but Bob Curran said to bring them uptown too and it would be all right. We had planned to have an oyster supper for the Prince at Jim Smith's hotel and then take him either to the Y.M.C.A. Pool Room or else to the tea social in the basement of the Presbyterian Church.

Unluckily, the Prince couldn't stay. It turned out that he had to get right back into his train and go on to Peterborough, Ontario, where they were to have a brass band to meet him, which naturally he didn't want to miss.

But the point is that it was a real welcome. And you could see that the Prince appreciated it. There was a warmth and a meaning to it that the Prince understood at once. It was a pity that he couldn't have stayed over and had time to see the carriage factory and the new sewerage plant. We all told the Prince that he must come back and he said that if he could he most certainly would. When the Prince's train pulled out of the station and we all went back uptown together (it was before prohibition came to Ontario) you could feel that the institution of royalty was quite solid in Orillia for a generation.

But you don't get that sort of thing in England. There's a formality and coldness in all their dealings with royalty that would never go down with us. They like to have the King come and open Parliament dressed in royal robes, and with a clattering troop of soldiers riding in front of him. As for taking him over to the Y.M.C.A. to play pin pool, they never think of it.

They have seen so much of the mere *outside* of his kingship that they don't understand the *heart* of it as we do in Canada.

But let us turn to the House of Commons: for no description of England would be complete without at least some mention of this interesting body. Indeed for the ordinary visitor to London the greatest interest of all attaches to the spacious and magnificent Parliament Buildings.

The House of Commons is commodiously situated beside the River Thames. The principal features of the House are the large lunch room on the western side and the tea-room on the terrace on the eastern. A series of smaller luncheon rooms extend (apparently) all round about the premises, while a commodious bar offers a ready access to the members at all hours of the day. While any members are in the bar a light is kept burning in the tall Clock Tower at one corner of the building, but when the bar is closed the light is turned off by whichever of the Scotch members leaves last.

There is a handsome legislative chamber attached to the premises from which – so the antiquarians tell us – the House of Commons took its name. But it is

43

not usual now for the members to sit in the legislative chamber as the legislation is now all done outside, either at the home of Mr. Lloyd George, or at the National Liberal Club, or at one or other of the newspaper offices. The House, however, is called together at very frequent intervals to give it an opportunity of hearing the latest legislation and allowing the members to indulge in cheers, sighs, groans, votes and other expressions of vitality. After having cheered as much as is good for it, it goes back again to the lunch rooms and goes on eating till needed again.

It is, however, an entire exaggeration to say that the House of Commons no longer has a real share in the government of England. This is not so. Anybody connected with the government values the House of Commons in a high degree. One of the leading newspaper proprietors of London himself told me that he had always felt that if he had the House of Commons on his side he had a very valuable ally. Many of the labour leaders are inclined to regard the House of Commons as of great utility, while the leading women's organizations, now that women are admitted as members, may be said to regard the House as one of themselves.

Looking around to find just where the natural service of the House of Commons comes in, I am inclined to think that it must be in the practice of "asking questions" in the House. Whenever anything goes wrong a member rises and asks a question. He gets up, for example, with a little paper in his hand, and asks the Government if ministers are aware that the Khedive of Egypt was seen yesterday wearing a Turkish tarbosh. Ministers say very humbly that they hadn't known it, and a thrill runs through the whole country.

The members can apparently ask any questions they like. In the repeated visits which I made to the gallery of the House of Commons I was unable to find any particular sense or meaning in the questions asked, though no doubt they had an intimate bearing on English politics not clear to an outsider like myself. I heard one member ask the Government whether they were aware that herrings were being imported from Hamburg to Harwich. The Government said no. Another member rose and asked the Government whether they considered Shakespeare or Molière the greatest dramatic artist. The Government answered that ministers were taking this under their earnest consideration and that a report would be submitted to Parliament.

Another member asked the Government if they knew who won the Queen's Plate this season at Toronto. They did – in fact this member got in wrong,

as this is the very thing that the Government do know. Towards the close of the evening a member rose and asked the Government if they knew what time it was. The Speaker, however, ruled this question out of order on the ground that it had been answered before.

The new education

"So you're going back to college in a fortnight," I said to the Bright Young Thing on the veranda of the summer hotel. "Aren't you sorry?"

"In a way I am," she said, "but in another sense I'm glad to go back. One can't loaf all the time."

She looked up from her rocking-chair with great earnestness.

How full of purpose these modern students are, I thought to myself. In my time we used to go back to college as to a treadmill.

"I know that," I said, "but what I mean is that college, after all, is a pretty hard grind. Things like mathematics and Greek are no joke, are they? In my day, as I remember it, we used to think spherical trigonometry about the hardest stuff of the lot."

She looked dubious.

"I didn't *elect* mathematics," she said.

"Oh," I said, "I see. So you don't have to take it. And what *have* you elected?"

"For this coming half semester – that's six weeks, you know – I've elected Social Endeavour."

"Ah," I said, "that's since my day; what is it?"

"Oh, it's *awfully* interesting. It's the study of conditions."

"What kind of conditions?" I asked.

"All conditions. Perhaps I can't explain it properly. But I have the prospectus of it indoors if you'd like to see it. We take up Society."

"And what do you do with it?"

"Analyse it," she said.

"But it must mean reading a tremendous lot of books."

"No," she answered. "We don't use books in this course. It's all Laboratory Work."

"Now I *am* mystified," I said. "What *do* you mean by Laboratory Work?"

"Well," answered the girl student with a thoughtful

look upon her face, "you see, we are supposed to break Society up into its elements."

"In six weeks?"

"Some of the girls do it in six weeks. Some put in a whole semester and take twelve weeks at it."

"So as to break it up pretty thoroughly?" I said.

"Yes," she assented. "But most of the girls think six weeks is enough."

"That ought to pulverize it pretty completely. But how do you go at it?"

"Well," the girl said, "it's all done with Laboratory Work. We take, for instance, department stores. I think that is the first thing we do, we take up the department store."

"And what do you do with it?"

"We study it as a Social Germ."

"Ah," I said, "as a Social Germ."

"Yes," said the girl, delighted to see that I was beginning to understand, "as a Germ. All the work is done in the concrete. The class goes down with the professor to the department store itself –"

"And then –"

"Then they walk all through it, observing."

"But have none of them ever been in a departmental store before?"

"Oh, of course, but, you see, we go as Observers."

"Ah, now I understand. You mean you don't buy anything and so you are able to watch everything?"

"No," she said, "it's not that. We do buy things. That's part of it. Most of the girls like to buy little knick-knacks, and anyway it gives them a chance to do their shopping while they're there. But while they *are* there they are observing. Then afterwards they make charts."

"Charts of what?" I asked.

"Charts of the employés; they're used to show the brain movement involved."

"Do you find much?"

"Well," she said hesitatingly, "the idea is to reduce all the employés to a Curve.'

"To a Curve?" I exclaimed. "An In or an Out?"

"No, no, not exactly that. Didn't you use Curves when you were at college?"

"Never," I said.

"Oh, well, nowadays nearly everything, you know, is done into a Curve. We put them on the board."

"And what is this particular Curve of the employé used for?" I asked.

"Why," said the student, "the idea is that from the Curve we can get the Norm of the employé."

"Get his Norm?" I asked.

"Yes, get the Norm. That stands for the Root Form of the employé as a social factor."

"And what can you do with that?"

"Oh, when we have that we can tell what the employé would do under any and every circumstance. At least that's the idea – though I'm really only quoting," she added, breaking off in a diffident way, "from what Miss Thinker, the Professor of Social Endeavour, says. She's really fine. She's making a general chart of the female employés of one of the biggest stores to show what percentage in case of fire would jump out of the window and what percentage would run to the fire escape."

"It's a wonderful course," I said. "We had nothing like it when I went to college. And does it only take in departmental stores?"

"No," said the girl, "the laboratory work includes ice-cream parlours as well."

"What do you do with *them*?"

"We take them up as Social Cells – Nuclei, I think the professor calls them."

"And how do you go at them?" I asked.

"Why, the girls go to them in little laboratory groups and study them."

"They eat ice-cream in them?"

"They *have* to ," she said, "to make it concrete. But while they are doing it they are considering the ice-cream parlour merely as a section of social protoplasm."

"Does the professor go?" I asked.

"Oh, yes, she heads each group. Professor Thinker never spares herself from work."

"Dear me," I said, "you must be kept very busy. And is Social Endeavour all that you are going to do?"

"No," she answered, "I'm electing a half-course in Nature Work as well."

"Nature Work? Well! Well! That, I suppose, means cramming up a lot of biology and zoology, does it not?"

"No," said the girl, "it's not exactly done with *books*. I believe it is all done by Field Work."

"Field Work?"

"Yes, Field Work four times a week and an Excursion every Saturday."

"And what do you do in the Field Work?"

"The girls," she answered, "go out in groups anywhere out of doors, and make a Nature Study of anything they see."

"How do they do that?" I asked.

"Why, they look at it. Suppose, for example, they come to a stream or a pond or anything –"

"Yes – "

"Well, they *look* at it."

"Had they never done that before?" I asked.

"Ah, but they look at it as a Nature Unit. Each girl

must take forty units in the course. I think we only do one unit each day we go out."

"It must," I said, "be pretty fatiguing work, and what about the Excursion?"

"That's every Saturday. We go out with Miss Stalk, the Professor of Ambulation."

"And where do you go?"

"Oh, anywhere. One day we go perhaps for a trip on a steamer and another Saturday somewhere in motors, and so on."

"Doing what?" I asked.

"Field Work. The aim of the course – I'm afraid I'm quoting Miss Stalk but I don't mind, she's really fine – is to break nature into its elements – "

"I see – "

"So as to view it as the external structure of Society and make deductions from it."

"Have you made any?" I asked.

"Oh, no" – she laughed – "I'm only starting the work this term. But, of course, I shall have to. Each girl makes at least one deduction at the end of the course. Some of the seniors make two or three. But you have to make *one*."

"It's a great course," I said. "No wonder you are going to be busy; and, as you say, how much better than loafing round here doing nothing."

"Isn't it?" said the girl student with enthusiasm in her eyes. "It gives one such a sense of purpose, such a feeling of doing something."

"It must," I answered.

"Oh, goodness," she exclaimed, "there's the lunch bell. I must skip and get ready."

She was just vanishing from my side when the Burly Male Student, who was also staying in the hotel, came puffing up after his five-mile run. He was getting himself into trim for enlistment, so he told me. He noted the retreating form of the college girl as he sat down.

"I've just been talking to her," I said, "about her college work. She seems to be studying a queer lot of stuff – Social Endeavour and all that!"

"Awful piffle," said the young man. "But the girls naturally run to all that sort of rot, you know."

"Now, your work," I went on, "is no doubt very different. I suppose you fellows have an awful dose of mathematics and philology and so on just as I did in my college days?"

Something like a blush came across the face of the handsome youth.

"Well, no," he said, "I didn't co-opt mathematics. At our college, you know, we co-opt two majors and two minors."

"I see," I said, "and what were you co-opting?"

"I co-opted Turkish, Music, and Religion," he answered.

"Oh, yes," I said with a sort of reverential respect, "fitting yourself for a position of choir-master in a Turkish cathedral, no doubt."

"No, no," he said, "I'm going into insurance; but, you see, those subjects fitted in better than anything else."

"Fitted in?"

"Yes. Turkish comes at nine, music at ten and religion at eleven. So they make a good combination; they leave a man free to – "

"To develop his mind," I said. "We used to find in my college days that lectures interfered with it badly. But now, Turkish, that must be an interesting language, eh?"

"Search me!" said the student. "All you have to do is answer the roll and go out. Forty roll-calls give you one Turkish unit – but, say, I must get on, I've got to change. So long."

I could not help reflecting, as the young man left me, on the great changes that have come over our

college education. It was a relief to me later in the day to talk with a quiet, sombre man, himself a graduate student in philosophy, on this topic. He agreed with me that the old strenuous studies seem to be very largely abandoned.

I looked at the sombre man with respect.

"Now your work," I said, "is very different from what these young people are doing – hard, solid, definite effort. What a relief it must be to you to get a brief vacation up here. I couldn't help thinking to-day, as I watched you moving round doing nothing, how fine it must feel for you to come up here after your hard work and put in a month of out-and-out loafing."

"Loafing!" he said indignantly. "I'm not loafing. I'm putting in a half summer course in Introspection. That's why I'm here. I get credit for two majors for my time here."

"Ah," I said, as gently as I could, "you get credit here."

He left me. I am still pondering over our new education. Meantime I think I shall enter my little boy's name on the books of Tuskegee College where the education is still old-fashioned.

Homer and Humbug

An academic suggestion

I do not mind confessing that for a long time past I have been very sceptical about the classics. I was myself trained as a classical scholar. It seemed the only thing to do with me. I acquired such a singular facility in handling Latin and Greek that I could take a page of either of them, distinguish which it was by merely glancing at it, and with the help of a dictionary and a pair of compasses whip off a translation of it in less than three hours. But I never got any pleasure from it. I lied about it.

I said to people who knew no Greek that there was a sublimity, a majesty about Homer which they could never hope to grasp. I said it was like the sound of the sea beating against the granite cliffs of the Ionian Esophagus, or words to that effect. As for the truth of it, I might as well have said that it was like the sound of a rum distillery running a nightshift on half-time. At any rate this is what I said about Homer, and when I spoke of Pindar – the dainty grace of his strophes – and Aristophanes – the delicious sallies of his wit, sally after sally, each sally explained in a note calling it a sally – I managed to suffuse my face with an animation which made it almost beautiful.

When I reflect that I have openly expressed regret, as a personal matter, even in the presence of women, for the missing books of Tacitus, and the entire loss of the Abracadabra of Polyphemus of Syracuse, I can find no words in which to beg for pardon. In reality I was just as much worried over the loss of the ichthyosaurus. More, indeed: I'd like to have seen it; but if the books Tacitus lost were like those he didn't, I wouldn't.

I believe all scholars lie like this. An ancient friend of mine, a clergyman, tells me that in Hesiod he finds a peculiar grace that he doesn't find elsewhere. He's a liar. That's all. Another man, in politics and in the legislature, tells me that every night before going to bed he reads over a page or two of Thucydides to keep his mind fresh. Either he never goes to bed or he's a liar. Doubly so: no one could read Greek at that frantic rate: and anyway his mind isn't fresh.

How could it be? he's in the legislature. I don't object to this man talking freely of the classics, but he ought to keep it for the voters. My own opinion is that before he goes to bed he takes whiskey: why call it Thucydides?

Be this as it may, I for my part bitterly regret the lies I have told about my appreciation of Latin and Greek literature. I am anxious to do what I can to set things right. I am therefore engaged on, indeed have nearly completed, a work which will enable all readers to judge the matter for themselves. What I have done is a translation of all the great classics, not in the usual literal way but on a design that brings them into harmony with modern life. I will explain what I mean in a minute. The translation is intended to be within reach of everybody.

My plan is so to transpose the classical writers as to give, not the literal translation word for word, but what is really the modern equivalent. Let me give an odd sample or two to show what I mean. Take the passage in the *First Book of Homer* that describes Ajax the Greek dashing into the battle in front of Troy. Here is the way it runs (as nearly as I remember) in the usual word-for-word translation of the classroom, as done by the very best professor, his spectacles glittering with the literary rapture of it.

Then he too Ajax on the one hand leaped (or possibly jumped) into the fight wearing on the other hand yes certainly a steel corslet (or possibly a bronze under-tunic) and on his head of course yes without doubt he had a helmet with a tossing plume taken from the mane (or perhaps extracted from the tail) of some horse which once fed along the banks of the Scamander (and it sees the herd and raises its head and paws the ground) and in his hand a shield worth a hundred oxen and on his knees too especially in particular greaves made by some cunning artificer (or perhaps blacksmith) and he blows the fire and it is hot. Thus Ajax leapt (or, better, was propelled from behind) into the fight.'

Now, that's grand stuff. There is no doubt of it. There's a wonderful movement and force to it. You can almost see it move, it goes so fast. But the modern reader can't get it. It won't mean to him what it meant to the early Greek. The setting, the costume, the scene has all got to be changed in order to let the reader have a real equivalent to judge just how good the Greek verse is. In my translation I alter it just a little, not much, but just enough to give the passage a form that reproduces the proper literary value of the verses, without losing anything of the majesty It describes, I may say, the Directors of the American Industrial Stocks rushing into the Balkan War cloud:

Then there came rushing to the shock of war
Mr. McNicoll of the C.P.R.
He wore suspenders and about his throat
High rose the collar of a sealskin coat,
He had on gaiters and he wore a tie,
He had his trousers buttoned good and high,
About his waist a woollen undervest
Bought from a sad-eyed farmer of the West,
(And every time he clips a sheep he sees
Some bloated plutocrat who ought to freeze),
Thus in the Stock Exchange he burst to view,
Leaped to the post, and shouted, "Ninety-two."

There! that's Homer, the real thing! Just as it sounded to the rude crowd of Greek peasants who sat in a ring and guffawed at the rhymes and watched the minstrel stamp it out into 'feet' as he recited it!

Or let me take another example from the so-called *Catalogue of the Ships* that fills up nearly an entire book of Homer. This famous passage names all the ships, one by one, and names the chiefs who sailed on them, and names the particular town or hill or valley that they came from. It has been much admired. It has that same majesty of style that has been brought to an even loftier pitch in the *New York Business Directory* and the *City Telephone Book*. It runs along, as I recall it, something like this:

And first indeed Oh yes was the ship of Homistogetes the Spartan, long and swift, having both its masts covered with cowhide and two rows of oars. And he, Homistogetes, was born of Hermogenes and Opthalmis and was at home in Syncope beside the fast flowing Paresis. And after him came the ship of Preposterus the Eurasian, son of Oasis and Hysterea.

. . . and so endlessly.
Instead of this I substitute, with the permission of the New York Central Railway, the official catalogue

of their locomotives taken almost word for word from the list compiled by their superintendent of works. I admit that he wrote in hot weather. Part of it runs:

Out in the yard and steaming in the sun
Stands locomotive engine number forty-one.
Seated beside the windows of the cab
Are Pat McGaw and Peter James McNab.
Pat comes from Troy and Peter from Cohoes,
And when they pull the throttle off she goes,
And as she vanishes there comes to view
Steam locomotive engine number forty-two.
Observe her mighty wheels, her easy roll,
With William J. Macarthy in control.
They say her engineer some time ago
Lived on a farm outside of Buffalo,
Whereas his fireman Henry Edward Foy
Attended school in Springfield, Illinois.
Thus does the race of man decay or rot:
Some men can hold their jobs and some can not.

Please observe that if Homer had actually written that last line it would have been quoted for a thousand years as one of the deepest sayings ever said. Orators would have rounded out their speeches with the majestic phrase, quoted in sonorous and unintelligible Greek verse, "some men can hold their jobs and some can not": essayists would have begun their most scholarly dissertations with the words, "It has been finely said by Homer that (in Greek) 'some men can hold their jobs' ": and the clergy in mid-pathos of a funeral sermon would have raised their eyes aloft and echoed, "Some men can not!"

This is what I should like to do. I'd like to take a large stone and write on it in very plain writing: "The classics are only primitive literature. They belong to the same class as primitive machinery and primitive music and primitive medicine," and then throw it through the windows of a University and hide behind a fence to see the professors buzz!

THE
GREAT
WAR

"ROULEZ, ROULANT, ROULEZ MA BOULE!"

eacock marked a turning point in Canadian humour. The old comic-valentine style disappeared and with it the puns and pointless misspelling, the dialect and the simply grotesque and ugly. Leacock had begun writing just before World War I, and he attained international fame in the postwar years. The war itself had brought other changes in humour. Until then, Canadians had managed to laugh during rebellions, wars, invasions and riots, but the joke had always been on the enemy. The Fenians, for instance, who had made a fumbling attempt to take over Canada in 1866, had been the objects of savage all-out humour.

Lizzie labours on the land;
What she does, I understand,
Is to make the cattle dizzy
Running around admiring Lizzie.

But in World War I, when, for the first time, war changed from something that often, through history, had resembled a comic opera, to a world-wide cataclysm that threatened universal annihilation, there was a change. The enemy was still occasionally the target of brutal humour (It's hard to imagine anyone laughing today at an essay such as one that ran in the *Maple Leaf*, a magazine put out in England for Canadian troops, in which a description of a sniper equipped with telescopic sights killing Germans was considered a warm bit of nonsense) but, in general, there was a shift away from the enemy and toward the average person caught up in a bewildering war. The humour of wartime civilians and life back back on the homefront made its appearance in the *Maple Leaf* which, for example, ran extracts from Correspondence on Separation Allowances and Pensions:

"You have changed my little girl into a little boy. Will it make any difference?"
"My Bill has been put in charge of a spittoon. Will I get more pay?"
"I have not received no pay since my husband was confined to a constipation camp in Germany."
"I am glad to tell you that my husband has now been repotted dead."
"If I don't get my husban 's money soon, I shall be obliged to go on the streets and lead an immortal life."

But, in a war bogged down in the trench mud, the main subject became the plight of the service man. It became the theme of a new kind of entertainment, entertainment for troops – and of one of Canada's best theatrical revues, The Dumbells. The group was formed by Captain M. W. Plunkett from frontline soldiers at Villiers Aux Bois in August 1917. The men performed by candlelight and gasoline-can spotlights, improvising props and stage sets. They wrote to London for costumes. Elsie Janiss, who was playing in *Hello America* with Maurice Chevalier, sent them some gowns. Ross Hamilton and Alan Murray, two ambulance men who had been in the first gas

HOW KLONDYKE BILL JOINED UP   (According to the artists, and according to fact)

Songs and skits of the beloved 'Dumbells'

attack at Ypres, dressed up as girls – a feature that was to remain a unique aspect of the show when it was reorganized after the war.

After the Armistice, the group tried out in the London (Ontario) Grand Theatre owned by Ambrose Small, and were booked immediately at the Grand Opera House in Toronto. They became a smash hit across Canada and the first Canadian revue to play Broadway.

To anyone in Canada over 50, the song *O What a Lovely War* conjures visions of the cockney Red Newman, lousy, muddy, in disreputable gear, who was the star of many Dumbell skits.

Lady at soldiers' convalescent hospital: Where were you wounded, young man?

Newman (leg propped up and wrapped in a quarter-mile of bandages): I was 'it in the 'ead, Ma'am, but the bandage slipped.

FRITZ THE FRIGHTFUL

The concert party that outlasted the war

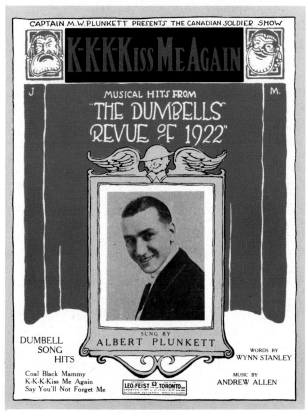

The sermon on Kit Inspection was written by one of the original group, a Winnipeg insurance salesman named Ted Charter. He came up with some truly ingenious ideas. One script which he wrote, and acted, was about scientists excavating Vimy Ridge in the year 2,000, turning up some bully beef and mistaking it for tile flooring. Charter also won the competition for the fastest and most efficient dresser of wounds in the Canadian Corps, and long after the war when he was making a hand-to-mouth living during the Depression, he invented a refrigerator with a telescoping shelf, a corn remover, and a carpet-cleaning formula, which he used to demonstrate in the home. "All he needed was the loan of a pail, brush and a pair of gloves to make himself thirty bucks," chuckles Jack Ayre, one of the show's originals.

Ayre, composer of the show's theme, *The Dumbell Rag,* which after the war sold, in sheet music, at the rate of 500 copies a performance, was the troupe's pianist; he started playing in "the pit" when it was a real pit dug out of the mud behind the lines at Vimy. Latterly, he plays the piano at Lions' Club luncheons and other gatherings around Toronto.

HIM OF HATE.

Kit inspection

BY TED CHARTER

(*Comes out dressed as curate, carrying pulpit and a phone book. Places the phone book on the pulpit. Music: "Drink to Me Only With Thine Eyes"*)
My text will be taken from the Book of Numbers, chapter seven, verse eleven (*makes motion of shooting craps*): At all times be ye prepared for no man knoweth when inspection cometh.

Then came one who stood erect and sounded a clarion that all men could hear. Then he that sounded the clarion departed and went his way and they that were gathered thereabout said:

"List! The clarion calleth us. We must go thither and assemble, for he who is chief among us would speak with us."

Behold, when they were thus assembled there came toward them one adorned with three golden stars (*points to epaulet*) who swaggereth much before men (*looks down at officers in the audience*). He of the three stars spoke to one man saying unto him, "Thou hast done well for all that was given thee thou still hast. How be it so?"

Then he that was spoken thus to said, "Sire, I am but newly in the land and am strange to the ways hereof."

Then he of the three stars spoke, saying unto them: "Which is the better man? He who doeth twice as much as he is asked or he that only doeth just as much as he is asked?"

And when they heard this, they were astonished and said: "He that doeth just as much as he is asked. He is the better man for he lasteth twice as longeth."

Then he of the three stars spoke unto another man and said unto him, "Where is the girdle that should surround thy waist (*makes motion indicating belt*) for he that is without a girdle when inspection cometh offendeth most grievously."

He that was spoken to looked sorely troubled and said. "Sire, only yesternight I loaned my girdle to another who went out visiting friends and his friends took him unto an inn and gave him to drink the juice of luscious grapes (*smacks lips*) –

"And he drank the juice –

"And he fell by the wayside and lay there as though slain, and behold a passerby wearing an armlet bearing two letters of red saw him and took compassion on him and lifteth him up and took him unto his house, yeah, verily, the house of detention."

Here endeth the reading of the lesson.

Official communiqué from the Front:
"Weather conditions reported favourable for observation."

Photographer (trying to be pleasant): "Back from the Front?"
Canadian (just arrived in England): "Say, you're clever if you can do that! Guess I'll just have a plain likeness took: none of your movies."

THE UNEASY YEARS

Goblin *was the sell-out smash hit of the Gay Twenties.*

When advertisers were kidded, some didn't see the joke.

From soon after the end of the Great War until the beginning of the Depression, there was a peculiar fad for college humour. Ordinarily, there's nothing funnier than the undergraduate humour when you're young, and nothing more awful when you're not. Its appreciation hinges on enthusiasm, brand-new muscles and fully functioning glands, and many a middle-aged journalist, looking back over things he forgot he wrote 40 years ago, when he was the funniest man on the campus, tries to forget them again for another 40 years at least. But they *were* funny at the time. Everything was funny, including a mysterious kind of writing like this from *Varsity*:

A MASQUE IN THREE TABLEAUX
(*Enter a corset attended by Mordecai the Midget who is being soundly laced*)
The Midget is a little man
You find him everywhere
You find too late he will not wait
To fill your tire with air.

But for a period of ten years or so, roughly corresponding to that between the appearance of the flapper and the heyday of the Charleston, college humour had such a vogue that it took a special place in the general field of humour. In 1921, four enterprising University of Toronto students launched a magazine called the *Goblin*, which sold out an hour and a half after it hit the newsstands, and soon had a bigger newsstand sale than any other magazine in Canada. Among its notable contributors was Richard Taylor, from Fort William, Ontario, who later became one of the best-known cartoonists in the United States and a regular contributor to the *New Yorker* magazine. He drew as many as eight cartoons per issue for the *Goblin,* using eight different techniques and eight different names. Another contributor was Lou Skuce, who later, as a well-known newspaper cartoonist, signed his drawings with a sketch of a goose ("Lou's goose" – get it?)

Goblin was one of the first publications with a sense of humour about advertising. Ford cancelled its account after *Goblin* ran the line " After three months all you have left is the payments," but other companies went along with the joke.

Regular standbys in the *Goblin* were hobos, drunks and bootleggers. One joke with endless variations went: "Does Mr. Jones, the college student, live here?" The next line was given by a Landlady, and she gave no end of answers (*e.g.*, "Yes, carry him in.") Much of the material was keyed to the New Woman, and seems humourless now, but it was timely and funny in the 1920s:

Legs

—by Mississippi   —Dedicated to Mr. Hippy.

Legs to the right of us
Legs to the left of us
Legs in front of us
How they display them.
On they go trippingly
Dainty and skippingly
Frost that bites nippingly
Does not dismay them.

Straight legs and bandy ones
Poor legs and dandy ones
Awkward and handy ones
Flirt with the breezes.
Round legs and flatter ones
Thin legs and fatter ones
Especially the latter ones
Showing their kneeses.

Knock-kneed and bony ones
Real legs and phony ones
Silk-covered tony ones
Second to none.
Straight and distorted ones
Mates and ill-sorted ones
Home and imported ones
Ain't we got fun.

'BOCKERS by Betty White

My love is quite slender,
   And graceful and sweet,
The girliest sort of girl
   One could meet;

BUT This morning I caught her,
   (My poor sainted aunts!)
Out taking the air,
   In a pair of tweed pants.

I was perfectly sober,
   Can't blame it on liquors,
My love was abroad,
   In black and white knickers.

I objected and stormed.
   We talked until night,
But "Knickers are swank,
   If your figure is right."

I called her —— —— ——
   (Excuse me for skipping),
I can't think it decent,
   But say—she looked ripping!

THE DOODADS
THE MAGIC APPLES
NOT A SINGLE CHRISTMAS GIFT HAS ANYBODY GIVEN ME. IT'S A CRUEL WORLD!
MERRY CHRISTMAS, NICKY! HERE'S A NICE BIG JUICY APPLE FOR YOU - AN' A NICE EASY JOB TOO!
JOB? FOR ME?
YES! YOURE JOB IS TO HAND OUT ONE APPLE TO EVERYBODY. TELL 'EM IT'S DOC'S CHRISTMAS GIFT
O-O-OH
BUT MIND THAT YOU GIVE 'EM ONE APPLE ONLY AND DON'T EAT MORE THAN ONE YOURSELF OR SOMETHING WILL HAPPEN TO YOU - THEY'RE MAGIC APPLES!
YEAH!
DOC'S FOOLIN' - I'LL EAT AS MANY APPLES AS I WANT TO. HERE'S TINY, I'LL GIVE HIM SOME, TOO
HA! HA! I KNEW DOC WAS ONLY FOOLIN'! AIN'T THESE APPLES GOOD TINY?
FOR GOODNESS SAKE!
HAR! HAR! TINY HAS SHRUNK TO A LITTLE TEENY WEENY!
OH DEAR! I'M SHRUNK TOO! DOC WASN'T FOOLIN'
HA, HA! POOR NICKY AND TINY! I'LL KEEP THEM LIKE THIS FOR AWHILE - IT WILL TEACH THEM NOT TO BE SELFISH!
MY STARS! WHAT'S HAPPENED YOU?
THEY WERE GREEDY AND ATE UP ALL DOC'S APPLES!
YEAH - AN' THEY WERE MAGIC APPLES
GR-R-!
HAR! HAR!
ARCH DALE

All this time, while adults were ogling short skirts and drinking bootleg gin, Canadians aged ten and under were reading about the *Doo Dads*. I could hardly believe it the other day when half a dozen people one after the other, said they had no idea what a *Doo Dad* was. Everybody who was anybody knew what *Doo Dads* were in the 1920s. They were little people with eyes like fried eggs and thimble-shaped horns, and if you were a kid in those days you wouldn't have minded being a *Doo Dad* yourself. These pot-bellied little figures – Doc Sawbones, Old Man Grouch, Flannelfeet the Cop – were created by Arch Dale, a political cartoonist with the *Grain Grower's Guide,* now the *Country Guide.* He was born in Dundee, Scotland, and worked on the Glasgow *News* and London *Comic Cuts* and *Funny Wonder* until the editor told him, according to his own account: "Dale, you're a failure. I'll give you fare to Canada. I'd rather make it Australia, but I can't afford it." Dale for a time was staff cartoonist with the Winnipeg *Free Press.* His favourite subject was Prime Minister Bennett. William Aberhart, Premier of Alberta, flew into a rage occasionally over Dale's cartoons. "He once called me a common drunkard," Dale said. "That was going too far. I didn't mind being called a drunkard. But he used the word 'common'." For four years, 1921 to 1925, Dale worked for a company in Chicago, when his *Doo Dads* were syndicated in fifty newspapers, including the Toronto *Sunday World.*

Canadians had just started to get over the war and enjoy the jazz age, when the Depression sobered them up. While middle-aged parents were still trying to get the hang of the Charleston, and having as much trouble as, a generation later, they were to have with the hula hoop – real-estate values collapsed, salaries were cut, people laid off and humour went into a slump. About the funniest thing that happened to anyone from then on was not to get fired. For thousands of unemployed there wasn't time to read humour. They read help-wanted ads – both of them – the one for a man with a bicycle to sell hand-cleaner on commission, and the other for a Hoffman press operator. They raced on their bikes to be the first to reach the potential employer, only to find 29 men there already, as if they'd materialized out of the sidewalk, and the job already taken. People sang songs as far from reality as they could get, like *Ramona* and *In a Little Spanish Town*; and the few jokes about panhandlers and hobo jungles weren't very funny.

One bright spot during the Depression was a half-page cartoon in the Toronto *Star Weekly* called *Birdseye Centre.* It was the creation of Jimmy Frise, a

59

Self-portrait by Jimmy Frise. For years he illustrated classic pieces written by chubby Greg Clark (below).

gentle, modest farmer's son from Port Perry, Ontario. For a quarter of a century it was one of the best-known and best-liked cartoons ever to appear in Canada. It was first called *Life's Little Comedies,* but quickly developed a population of rural characters – Pigskin Peters, Ely, whose wife did all the work, the autocratic captain of the lake ferry, Old Archie and his tame moose. *Birdseye Centre* ran for more than 25 years, and for a short time, before Frise's death, appeared as *Juniper Junction* in the Montreal *Standard,* which later became *Weekend* Magazine. During the Depression years, Greg Clark, a Toronto *Star* reporter and later a war correspondent, who had been writing humour pieces for the *Star Weekly,* began to write a weekly full-page story, illustrated by Jimmy Frise, which dealt with all kinds of predicaments, many of which Clark and Frise created themselves. Clark is still one of Canada's most entertaining talkers. Recently he revealed that he had taken Ernest Hemingway aside when Hemingway worked for the *Star,* and told him, "You'll never get anywhere with all those damned little short sentences." The stories he did with Jimmy Frise weren't always, or even often, as funny in print as the way he told them to his friends. One time he and Frise bought a park bench, kept the receipt, carried it to Queen's Park and sat on it waiting for a mounted policeman to ride by – a particularly handsome, arrogant one they'd been laying for. As soon as they were sure he'd seen them, they picked up the bench and started to walk away with it. When the cop galloped up in a rage, they told him it was theirs, such an apparent lie that he took them both down to the police station, where they produced the bill of sale.

One of the reasons for the popularity of Jimmy Frise's *Birdseye Centre* was that, as Canada became more industrialized, and more and more people crowded into the cities, they began to think nostalgically and romantically of the country. They liked to

read about the country, while in the city, and it provided some of our best writing. Ever since the early 1900s, Peter McArthur, the son of a homesteader near London, Ontario, who began his career as a journalist selling jokes and cartoon ideas to the humour magazines, including *Grip,* had been writing gently humorous essays for the Toronto *Globe* and the *Farmer's Advocate.* Many of these appeared in book form. McArthur probably wrote more about cows than anyone in history – optimistic cows, defeatist cows, sick cows and thoughtful cows. His descriptions were nonetheless entertaining for telling more about McArthur than they did about cows.

A few days ago we had an ideal shower, warm, still and occasionally shot with sunshine . . . I had to turn out the cows for a drink, and the day seemed to suit them exactly. While old Fenceviewer was waiting to have her stall cleaned and her bed made up she humped her back against the shower and chewed her cud, and if she could have had a couple of hands stuck into pockets she would have made a perfect picture of contentment.

Cows are deep

Cows are deep. They think thoughts that are beyond the poets . . . but only when they have the proper environment. They don't think all over the place like college professors and eminent people generally. Cows can spend days and days without thinking, but when the conditions are right they think unutterable things, and the object that inspires them to their loftiest flights is a gate. But it is not enough to have a cow see a gate to start her thinking. You must try to drive her through it. In fact, I am not sure that one lone cow would start thinking even in a gate. You must have a herd of them and it usually works out in about this way. After you have run yourself out of breath gathering the herd the boss will take the lead and the skittish young cattle will be bringing up the rear. As soon as the boss gets into the gate where none of the others can pass her a great idea will strike her and she will stop to chew her cud and think it over. If you are in a hurry you will probably start yelling at her, but it will do no good. Nothing can interrupt her profound thoughts and your yelling will only disturb the young cattle and start them scampering around the field. In all probability you will start throwing clods and sticks, and if your aim is good you may jolt her though the gate, but you will find that before further progress can be made you will have to gather the young cattle again. When you get your little flock to the gate once more you will find that the deputy boss becomes seized of a great idea when she reaches the middle, and the business of yelling, throwing clods, and gathering the young cattle has to be done all over again.

There have been times when it has taken me half an hour to get a thoughtful herd of cows through a twelve-foot gate. Still, I always solace myself with the reflection that I have been the first to discover that cows think.

But gates are not the only things that inspire cows. Doors also seem to have a very stimulating effect on their cerebral processes. Sometimes when I turn the cows out to water I just go down the line unloosing their chains. When the first cow reaches the door and gets a glimpse of the fair round world she stops to reflect on its beauty. The cows behind her, lacking this inspiration, begin to hook and bunt one another until the stable is a howling pandemonium, but the cow in the door is in no wise disturbed. She stands there and thinks, and thinks, and thinks.

The Farrow Cow

BY PETER McARTHUR

The calf belonged to the purposeful and strong-minded red cow. Of course, she was very proud of her calf, and mooed solicitously when we approached to examine it. But strange to say she was not nearly so excited about it as her oldest daughter, a quiet and hitherto well-behaved cow that has been milking all winter and in farrow this season. Judging from her actions she had adopted the new calf, and had taken out adoption papers before we arrived on the scene. She ran around and bawled and acted silly as soon as I began to push the calf towards the barn. By the way, pushing a young calf that braces its front legs and insists on lying down every couple of rods while its real mother and an idiotic farrow cow are threatening to run over you all the time, is a job that is rather trying on the temper. But I finally got it through the gate, and proceeded to push it along towards the drive-shed where I could get it out of sight.

The mother objected, of course, and bawled her protest as loudly and ineffectively as a loyal Opposition when a Government is putting through a railway subsidy. But the farrow cow made as much noise as a self-elected reformer. She stood by the gate and pumped up basso-profundo bawls from her second or lower stomach. Every time she bawled she humped her back and moved her tail up and down like the handle of an old-fashioned wooden pump. But I paid no attention to her. I could not see where her feelings were being lacerated, and I kept right on picking up the calf and setting him on his wobbly legs and pushing him towards the drive-shed.

Just as I reached the door and the calf had gone down again I was startled by a yell behind me. I turned hastily, just in time to see the farrow cow in the act of shredding herself through a tight barbed wire fence. I was too late to head her off, and, as I watched her struggles. I felt that when she got through she would be of no use for anything but Hamburg steak, and I reflected with some satisfaction that the new onions in the garden are ready to be used for a meat garnish. But when she got through she did not sink on the earth in a pile of little pieces as I expected, but ran like a deer, bawling like a foghorn, to where a calf that had been weaned the day before was bleating for its mother. By this time the red cow had become excited and was threatening to follow her fool daughter through the barbed wire fence. And the cow whose calf had been taken the day before also went into hysterics.

I don't believe there was ever so much noise and excitement on the farm as there was for the next few minutes. The boy kept the red cow from going through the fence, and I opened the door of the drive-shed and hurled the calf under the buggy, where it lay down once more with a little grunt of satisfaction. Then I went after the farrow cow to see how much she was damaged. It seemed incredible, but there was not a scratch visible on her silly carcass. Now, will some learned man please explain how that could be possible? Whenever I try to go through a barbed wire fence, even though I go at it with the greatest circumspection and care, the barbs catch in my hat, coat, trousers and stockings, and even catch the rag on my sore finger – not to mention the bias patches they tear out of the most sensitive skin in Middlesex County. And yet that cow ripped through that fence by brute force and didn't get a scratch that was visible to the naked eye.

Before I got peace restored on the place I had to capture each cow and lead her into the stable. I had to put in the three of them before they would stop threatening to commit hari-kari on the barbed wire fence. As I think over the occurrence the lesson that sticks in my mind is that the farrow cow was wonderfully like a professional reformer. Though her interests were not involved in any way, she made a bigger disturbance and got more thoroughly worked up than the cow that was really bereaved. And nobody thanked her or gave her a word of praise. I admit that this lesson came home to me with great force.

BACK TO BULLETS

The Depression never ended: it was replaced by World War II. Except for imitations of Hitler, wartime humour was now almost exclusively about life in the services. One of the most inept, popular and best-known soldiers in the Canadian Army was a fictional character named "Turvey" from Skookum Falls, B.C., created by Earle Birney, a poet and professor of English at the University of British Columbia. Turvey had some amusing, and many appalling, traits. One side of his character that stirred reminiscences in anyone who went through the Depression was the background of jobs he held before enlisting.

Turvey

BY EARLE BIRNEY

The Personnel Corporal was a bulky balding chap whose questions came out tonelessly between sucks on a rooty pipe.

"Born thirteenth May nineteen-twenty-two Skookum Falls, B.C. . . . white single next of kin Mr. Leopold Turvey Skookum Falls brother. No glasses right-handed. Ussssp?"

Turvey would not have ventured to halt the flow of the voice and bulbous pen if he had not decided that the last suck of the corporal's pipe was meant to be a question mark.

"Lefthanded, sir . . . except for hockey."

The corporal's pen wavered and his pipe hissed mildly.

"Wut about a rifle,"

Turvey smiled ingratiatingly. "Anyway you like, sir."

"Wotcha chief occupation civil life?"

Turvey thought carefully. "Well, I was choker-man in the Kootenays once. Just a two-bit camp." The corporal looked blank. "Then I was a bucker in Calgary."

"You mean you was a bronco-buster?" The edge in the corporal's voice betrayed a hint of unprofessional surprise.

"No, s – , no, corporal, on a bridge. You know – holdin' a bat under the girder for the riveter. I was

"For the last time. . . . cut out that 'Quack, quack' stuff."

"Herbie," the Maple Leaf's *dumb cluck in the rear rank, was the despair of the sergeant and the delight of the private soldiery. You couldn't call him smart, but you noticed that he was never late for chow.*

a sticker too." The corporal kept his eyes on the form, nodding as if he had known all along, but his bald head pinkened slightly and his pen halted. "That's fine. How long you, uh, stick?"

"At stickin'? Not very long. I got to missin' rivets with my bucket and a hot one set a big Swede on fire and he complained to the strawboss. Then I rode the rods east and sorta bummed. Then I was a scurfer in a coke plant. And I was a pouncer once, for a while."

The corporal twisted his ear as if he were having trouble hearing. His face had become a mask of distrust. Turvey felt sorry he had mentioned pouncing and he added apologetically:

"In a hat factory, Guelph. You know – sandpaperin' up the fuzz on fedoras."

But the corporal had taken the pipe out of his mouth and was holding it at a monitory angle, and his voice was a growl:

"Dont try no smart stuff here. I ast you wut cher chief occupation was. Wut did you do longest?"

Turvey thought rapidly. There was the time he was a popsicle-coater, and then assistant flavour-mixer in that candy factory. But he quit after, what was it, four months, got tired of the vanilla smell always on his clothes. Wanted to get east anyway and try the army again. The corporal was staring sullenly at his forms. What happened then? O yes, the army turned him down because he had a mess of hives and his front teeth were out and his feet kind of flat. So after a while he landed that tannery job. How long was he there? Gee, almost a whole winter!

"Wet-splittin'."

The corporal's eyes rose, speckled and malevolent, but they saw only a round face beaming with the pleasure of recall and the tremulous smile of the young man anxious to please.

"I ran a machine scrapin' fat off hides. Eastern Tannery, Montreal."

The corporal laid his pipe down (it had gone out), wrote "Machine Operator," and asked hurriedly:

"Any previous military experience?"

"Well, we started cadets in Kuskanee High but we never got rifles. But I was in the Boy Sc – "

"That's all. Wait on a bench atta back till the officer calls you, next man!" The corporal looked past him, mopped his veined head with a khaki handkerchief and whanged his pipe spitefully against the table leg.

THE PIN UPS

Wings, the World War II air force magazine, ran stories of Gremlins (the mysterious beings who played tricks like letting oil out of airplane engines), pictures of the moustache of the year, cartoons of mother birds booting fledglings out of the nests, and lots of photographs of Dorothy Lamour, Lana Turner, Jane Russell, Gene Tierney and Susan Hayward, all decorously clad (by today's standards), or of girls pertly uniformed.

One contributor to *Wings* was Sgt. Eric Nicol, who was to become a syndicated columnist, and three-time winner of the Leacock Medal for Humour.

WINGS

THE LOG OF THE R.C.A.F.

"...HE LOVES ME, HE LOVES ME NOT..."

"YOU'RE A HELLUVA NAVIGATOR! DOES THIS LOOK LIKE GOOSE BAY?"

"N ABOUT HIS 48 AGAIN, SIR. HE
N PROVE HIS GRANDMOTHER DIED."

PILOTS -------
WHEN BAILING OUT
DON'T FORGET YOUR
BOMB-AIMER!

"OU SHOULD HAVE THOUGHT OF THAT BEFORE WE CAME UP"

Wings *flew out of Ottawa to all ranks of the R.C.A.F.
By later standards the pin-ups were cover-ups. One
editor remembers, "the only flying we did was up
Elgin Street" but the editor's chair launched
several writers into big careers in post war years.*

"Oh fine, now we're gonna play games."

FLOGG & THE ERKS

BY ·ERIC NICOL

I was apathetic toward the idea of parading in my summer issue because it would mean buttoning the pants at the neck. Usually we fellows like to affect a nonchalant, careless air around the hangar by wearing our pants open at the neck, in accordance with Goonsbury's unwritten code for ground-crew erks, namely: one button undone means that the wearer works on twin-motor aircraft, while all the buttons undone mean that he is absent-minded as hell.

The following morning, therefore, I fell under the scrutiny of Sgt. Flogg, who was favouring us with a slight pre-inspection inspection behind the hangar.

"Will the uniform lurking in the third rank kindly fall out," he crooned softly.

I fell out. Sgt. Flogg strolled up to me slowly, a ghastly grin etched on his strictly issue face. He looked me all over with a daft, eager expression, then cawed: "Come out, come out, wherever you are!"

I stuck my head over the top of the pants, blinking in the bright sunlight. He jumped back like a startled moose.

"Good gawd!" he yelled, "There's a man in there!"

A half-hearted cheer went up from the flight. Flogg approached me again, feigning an amazed interest.

"Comfy?" he murmured, pinching my cheek.

I kept watching his feet, having read somewhere that it was the best way to anticipate a blow. He walked around me, his head cocked on one side.

"Anything to declare?" he asked in a hollow voice, and I realized he must be peering into the depths of the seat of my pants. "Any cameras? Stolen tyres? A civilian, perhaps?"

I waited grimly.

Sgt. Flogg put his arm around my shoulders affectionately, turning to face the flight. When he spoke, his voice was low and rich, and it shook a little.

"This," he said, "this is victory through air power."

There was a smattering of applause.

"You will notice how well this man is camouflaged," he continued. "You would never think to look at him that he was an airman, would you?"

General shaking of heads.

"Look at them buttons!" he went on passionately. "They're so dirty the eagles is flying on instruments!"

He turned to face me once more.

"We're not keeping you up, are we?" he purred.

I shook my head, causing my cap to ground-loop prettily.

"THEN WHAT THE HELL IS KEEPING YOU UP?" he bellowed, spinning the prop badges on my arm.

I retracted my head into my pants hastily, drooping back to my place in the rear rank.

Sgt. Flogg was now prepared to move us off.

"Squaw, atten-Hup!" he erupted.

He fastened me with a steely glare again.

"Didn't you hear me say 'atten-Hup!?" he demanded thickly.

"Yes, Sergeant," I replied sympathetically. "Have you ever thought of trying *Tums*? They say they're wonderful for acid indigestion. Burps to you."

"And nuts to you!" screamed Flogg.

This remark was rather uncharitable of Sgt. Flogg, I thought, seeing as it was common knowledge that all his commands sounded like symptoms of after-dinner distress. We heard he had been posted from Y Depot because he burped in front of his flight waiting to embark and it had quick-marched right off the end of the pier.

He was obliged to retire from action, however, as the officers marched to their posts. Eventually, after the squadron had been dressed and undressed more times than Gypsy Rose Lee, we moved off.

Disaster struck at me almost immediately. Crossing a street-car track in mid-town, my foot caught in a rail and I was obliged to follow the car line to an east-end car barn, where a near-sighted mechanic attempted to grease my bearings. I hardly enjoyed the whole thing at all.

like now

THE MANY FUNNY FACES OF

Modern is a relative term that can apply to the period since the Middle Ages, or to the past ten years, or, if you're under 12, to the last two years, but in relation to humour in Canada, it seems to best fit the period from around the time of World War II until the present. The Bomb had left a new world that nobody was quite sure about. Morals, political philosophy and religion were in a state of suspension, and humour became more satir-irical, disrespectful, cynical and pointed.

Spring Thaw introduced a new kind of fast-paced satirical review, spoofed royalty for the first time, and inspired a succession of small reviews keyed to caustic commentary on current affairs. Canada produced some of its most outstanding radio talent; TV brought new humour techniques, talent and abuses. The late show *Nightcap* kept people wide awake at midnight with bawdy slapstick and caused one American in Detroit to write in: "Did I really see what I think I just saw!"

The post-war years brought an influx of some of our most brilliant magazine and newspaper writers from abroad. Duncan Macpherson's cartoons began to reach out of the pages of *Maclean's* and belt people.

Humour that relied on racial prejudice vanished and humour directed *at* racial prejudice appeared.

Sex, which had come out in the open between the wars, now became such a charter member of the establishment and the subject of such snobbery that people began to be shocked by words like "modesty" and "virtue." All in all, humour began to depend more on spontaneous mirth than on preconceived notions of what should be funny. There was more variety and greater extremes. Humour was either better than it had been, or worse than it ever had been, but more often than not it was better.

In the late 1940s, as Canadians entered the long traffic jams that appear to be the permanent lot of urban man, commuters in line-ups of stalled cars heard over their car radios the voice of a kindly, cactus-voiced old timer named Rawhide who gave the feeling that he was leaning on a pitchfork and talking around a cud of tobacco, yet who had cosy interviews with such celebrities as Winston Churchill – who apparently was always available for a morning chat in a C.B.C. sound booth in Toronto. All this emanated from a handsome young man of 26 named Max

MAX "RAWHIDE" FERGUSON

Ferguson, a C.B.C. staff announcer with a remarkably inventive mind and a gift for imitating the voice of anyone he happened to feel like interviewing. He sat in a broadcasting booth not much bigger than a phone booth providing his own sound effects, and coping with a weird assortment of characters of his invention – an insufferable pedant named Marvin Mellowbell, a loud-mouthed ignoramus named Stupid, who hated Rawhide, and Grandma, a sweet little old lady who was always trying to get Rawhide to eat poison chocolates. People estimated Ferguson's age between 75 and 100.

Several public figures blasted out at Rawhide. Douglas G. Ross, then Progressive Conservative M.P. for Toronto St. Paul's, defined Ferguson's antics as "that programme of meaningless raving and tripe, couched in the poorest possible illiterate English, known as *After Breakfast Breakdown*, which is an insult to the intelligence of the Canadian people." Reverend Stuart Iveson, of the First Baptist Church in Ottawa, accused the C.B.C. of "sacrilege, blasphemy, evil, public avowal of irreligion and something that Godless Soviet Russia could hardly improve upon,"

which made even more Canadians tune in ...to Rawhide.

Around the same time Tommy Tweed, a former science student at the University of Manitoba, who wrote a number of satirical sketches for radio, adapted for radio the poems of 'Sarah Binks', which had been written as a spoof of high-brow literary criticism by Paul Hiebert, a chemistry professor. Hiebert managed to get a lot of fun out of simply putting Sarah's literary efforts in a rural setting; or rather having her write poetry out of just about anything she found lying around the farm, and just missing her effects, all of which Hiebert made worse with his running literary commentary. Of Sarah's love song, *High on a Cliff*, for instance, which ends with the lines

"Three fountain pens, where the ripples run,
A trick cigarette case and a package of gum;
With leaden eyes I watched my Love drift by,
And watched the ripples blending with the sky,"

Hiebert wrote: "It is not Sarah at her absolute best. But on the other hand it is not Sarah at her absolute worst."

69

SARAH BINKS

PAUL HIEBERT

It's a joy again, for spreading time has found me,
Within my own paternal field and fold;
It's spreading time, and once more all around me
The air is rich, and fields are flecked with gold;
From yonder heap the busy sparrow flutters,
To other heaps, and all the heaps surveys;
And from the dump the barnyard chicken mutters,
And rooster lifts his solemn voice in praise.
Alas, that winter's heavy cloak should ever
Enfold this scene in dreary white, and bring
The golden spots that mark our high endeavour,
Beneath its blighted snow bands until springs;
But spring will come, and what today we harrow,
Will reappear, for spring makes all things new,
The shovel and the stone-boat and the barrow,
And what we spread will once more come to view.

Oh, I heard your voice at daybreak,
Calling loud and sweet and clear;
I was hiding in the turnips
With a cricket in my ear;
A miller-moth in one ear,
And a cricket in the other,
But I heard your dear voice calling
To the piglets and their mother;
Heard your own voice rising, falling,
Loud and long and sharp and shrill,
Calling "Sooky, Sooky, Sooky!"
To the piglets on the hill;
"Hi, Sooky, Ho, Sooky,
Come and get your swill!"

The farmer and the farmer's wife
Lead frolicsome and carefree lives,
And all their work is but in play,
Their labours only exercise.
The farmer leaps from bed to board,
And board to binder on the land;
His wife awakes with shouts of joy,
And milks a cow with either hand.
Then all in fun they feed the pigs,
And plough the soil in reckless glee,
And play the quaint old-fashioned game
Of mortgagor and mortgagee.
And all day long they dash about,
In barn and pasture, field and heath;
He sings a merry roundelay,
She whistles gaily through her teeth.
And when at night the chores are done,
And hand in hand they sit and beam,
He helps himself to applejack,
And she to Paris Green.

John Drainie holds up the wall of the barber shop in Crocus, Sask., in one of W.O. Mitchell's serials, Jake and the Kid.

W.O. Mitchell's stories about life on the Prairies, *Jake and the Kid*, first appeared in *Maclean's* then became, for many years, popular C.B.C. weekly radio and TV shows, with John Drainie playing the part of Jake, the crochety, tale-spinning hired man. Mitchell, wrote sensitively and dramatically of the Prairies, of flowers, sky, sunsets, grain fields, droughts and blizzards. To the joy of thousands of Canadians, he managed to weave this feeling into homespun nonsense like:

Why I never fergit the winter of o'six. So cold you could see jack rabbits clear across the prairie – froze. Froze in the middle of the air, height about two foot off of the ground where they leapt and got froze. One day I seen a jack kinda squatted over a rose apple bush, about three feet behind him a coyote with his feet drawed up right under him ready to spring on the jack. Come spring the jack he unfroze first; gotta head start on the coyote that way. Same winter the Fister boys caught them a young coyote; trained him to howl tenor so's he could carry the harmony.

Spring Thaw, Canada's longest running review, was founded by Mavor Moore in 1948 almost by accident as a last-minute replacement when a script failed to turn up for a play that was to be held by the New Play Society in the basement auditorium of the Royal Ontario Museum in Toronto. Moore and the group turned out a complete review in two nights to save the rental deposit on the theatre. The curtain went up on schedule, but Moore was sure the show would be a fiasco. Instead, it got enthusiastic reviews, and sold out the theatre the second night. Since then it has presented in each yearly edition the material of dozens of Canadian writers. One of the most consistent and one of the best contributors was Moore himself who wrote, among other things, *Togetherness*, a song sung by a cardinal, an Anglican archbishop, an orthodox patriarch and a United Church moderator.

71

Spring Thaw presents satirical writing from dozens of Canadians. This cast centred on Jane Mallett (under table).

togetherness

BY MAVOR MOORE

ARCHBISHOP:
We've recently been holding private meetings . . .
CARDINAL:
Merely to exchange fraternal greetings . . .
PATRIARCH:
And see what possibility there was . . .
MODERATOR:
Of getting together once again – because . . .
ALL FOUR:
The issues seem so trivial that divide us
Compared with those attacking from outside us.
Western civilization may
Be near the end of its tether:
And that's why we are here to say
It's time we got together.
Togetherness! Togetherness!
All praise to brotherly love!
The churches will soon coalesce
If we keep talking of
Togetherness! Togetherness!
Toge-e-etherness!

Quartet in Togetherness *(from left) — Dave Broadfoot, Jack Duffy, Peter Mews and Bill Cole.*

CARDINAL:
You may find a prelate too much of a zealot
But the trouble with other religions has been
They will not concede that the Catholic creed
Is the only escape from Original Sin.
You may think the Vatican very dogmatic
And strict in its doctrine – Well, maybe it is:
But God allows others to go their own way,
While we are infallibly going in His.

ALL FOUR:
But still we bless Togetherness,
All praise to brotherly love . . . etc.

ARCHBISHOP:
An Archbishop mustn't relent – and he doesn't
In spreading the gospel within his own see:
And that involves routing the low churches out
And keeping the monarchy still C. of E.
But High Church adherents are warned that our way
Is dead against vulgar religious display:
For God is a gentleman through and through,
And in all probability Anglican too.

ALL FOUR:
But still we bless Togetherness,
All praise to brotherly love . . . etc.

PATRIARCH:
In Orthodox litany we can't admit any
Further political woes than we have;
So we avoid feuds by a rule that precludes
A Greek or a Serb contradicting a Slav.
It would take hours to chronicle all the canonical
Differences between us and the rest;
But we'd have you recall that though God made us all
He incontrovertibly made us the best.

ALL FOUR:
But still we bless Togetherness,
All praise to brotherly love . . . etc.

MODERATOR:
United Church pastors are always past-masters
Whenever a compromise needs to be found;
And frankly who cares to split biblical hairs
So long as your morals are perfectly sound?
Our flocks are enormous, and all noncomformist,
Our virtuous conduct all others' excels:
We have God's guarantee that our conscience is free,
And we won't take our orders from anyone else.

ALL FOUR:
But still we bless Togetherness!
All praise to brotherly love!
Our efforts will meet with success
If we keep singing of
Togetherness! Togetherness!
Toge-e-etherness!

Corinne Conley: "Poor, poor, Dick."

Dick and Jane
BY GERRY ROSS AND MARLENE PERRY

(A little girl with a big book. She reads haltingly.)

Look Dick, look Jane. See the hydrogen bomb drop: drop, drop, drop. Who has dropped the bomb?

Where is the button, Mother asks? Here is the button, says Father. Here, here, here. Someone has pushed the button.

Who has pushed the button? Sally says Spot has pushed the button. Spot says Sally has pushed the button. Jack says Niki has pushed the button. Dick pushed the button. He thought it was the light switch. He did not want light; he wanted to rest, but there *was* light, and he *did* rest. Poor, poor Dick.

Look Jane, look Tom, see the guided missile . . . follow father down the street. See Father run. Run, run, run. Poor, poor Father.

Dick and Jane are playing house . . . see the fall-out shelter grow. Grow, grow, grow. Look Dick, here comes another bomb. See the fallout shelter fall. Fall, fall, fall. Now father is gone, mother is gone, Dick is gone. Sally is gone, Jane is gone, Spot is gone.

Who is left?

Puff!

73

The comics who stayed at home

Frank Shuster (left) and Johnny Wayne began an international career as funnymen with their show The Brown Pumpernickel.

Two of the busiest and best-known students at the University of Toronto in mid-Depression years, were a couple of friends from Harbord Collegiate named John Wayne and Frank Shuster. They wrote parodies for a column called "Champus Cat" in the *Varsity* ("Sure we're old newspaper men. But we quit. There's no money in old newspapers."). They wrote, staged and took part in the University College Follies. They were on a radio show called *The Wife Preservers*. They were serious students who practically lived in libraries studying for master's degrees in English, but their academic background, as publicity for a future comedy team, couldn't have been better if it had been planned by a press agent.

Their literacy gave them more than an identity, it provided them with the form and substance of much of their material. Their slapstick has high literary overtones. In their skit of a Shakespearean ball game, they wrote, with the ear of a poet, "Hark, the players come. To our appointed places shall we go. You at first and I behind the plate." In their parody of Julius Caesar, a private eye says "Now where's the corpus delicti?" "The what?" "The corpus delicti. Whatsamatter? Don't you understand plain Latin?" Even in their early years they wrote jokes that, if they didn't scan like Virgil, at least had a certain poetic rhythm. Even their hobos had a finely tuned ear for the English language. "Pardon me, do you have twenty cents for a cup of coffee?" "Coffee's only a dime." "I know, won't you join me?"

Their literate quality never left them during their days as servicemen when they wrote, staged and starred in the Army Show, nor, after the war, when they became well-known on radio and television. It came into full bloom when they appeared on Ed Sullivan's show in *Rinse the Blood off My Toga*. One of their jokes immediately went the rounds of the New York bars: "Give me a martinus." "You mean a martini." "When I want two I'll ask for them." Another joke from this show that made a hit was the wail of Caesar's widow: "I told him. I *told* him. I said, 'Julie *don't go!*' "

Since then Wayne and Shuster have made it big in the U.S., but they still stay in Canada, because they like it in Canada. They get humour out of that, too. Once, they claim, when they explained to a hard-pressing agent that they stayed in Canada because they were happy there, liked hockey, liked their friends, in fact were contented in Canada, he moaned in desperation, "Happiness isn't everything." Wayne and Shuster apparently think it is. Now that they're at the top, they make fewer shows than they could, even less money than they could, to keep it that way.

The "Mad Professor" – done in fright wig – is one of Wayne's favourite characterizations. They steer clear of satire or anything "beyond the fringe."

They make Return of the Son of Tarzan, *complete with nubile jungle maid. They write their own scripts, with Shuster usually playing it square and straight.*

75

A foretaste of hindsight

BY TOMMY TWEED

General Director of the C.B.C., to Junior Producer who is trying to sell the story of Little Red Riding Hood: Now there is nothing between you and the programme but checking it with the Provinces to see how they react. If you can ever get them to agree, we'll put it on.

Junior Producer. Oh sir, you have given me renewed hope. I will travel across Canada and get them to help me.
General Director: Brave boy. Check with me when you get back.
Junior Producer: I will. Please wish me luck.
General Director: Oh I do, with all my heart.
Junior Executive: Then shake.
General Director: I wish I could, but my hands are tied.
    (Music: Off to see Canada, starting at the West Coast.)

Junior Producer: . . . And that's my story. Will you, as British Columbia Representatives, agree to the story of *Little Red Riding Hood?*
B.C.: I'm sorry, Junior, but if you've read our magazine advertising, you'll know that so much business is moving to B.C. that there just isn't time for *Little Red Riding Hood.*
Junior: But, Sir . . .
B.C.: And even if there were time, you would have to cut out all reference to the woodchoppers who saved her. We've had enough trouble in the Lumber Business already.

Alberta: Now just run over the end of the story again.
Junior: Well, just as the wicked wolf was about to eat little Red Riding Hood, in came the brave wood choppers and caught him in the act.
Alberta: Ah yes, have you checked that with the Supreme Court?
Junior: What?
Alberta: The Act, of course.
Junior: But this was an Act of Mercy.
Alberta: Makes no difference. We got caught with an Act once; never again.

Saskatchewan:
We attack the cost of living in Saskatchewan
By cooperating, which is how we all get on

We're even organized to try
To make it cheaper when you die
In the flat and fertile Province of Saskatchewan.
Junior: That's very nice, but are none of the men home today.
Sask: Nope. All out hunting. Nice weather for it, too. Clear and Coldwell.

Junior: Excuse me, but what are you going to do about my broadcast of *Little Red Riding Hood?*
Man: I'd like to help you, Junior, but we in Manitoba don't like that reference to the wolf at the end of the story.

Ontario: Welcome to Ontario.
Junior: Oh, I'm not a tourist. I came to see what you think of *Little Red Riding Hood.*
Ontario: What's her background? Did her father attend Upper Canada College?
Junior: There's no mention of her father.
Ontario: Pity.
Junior: No, just her mother.
Ontario: U.E.L.?
Junior: The story doesn't say.
Ontario: I'm beginning to think very little of this story.
Junior: Me, too.

Quebec: Is it that you wish to see me, Monsieur?
Junior: Yes. As a Junior Producer from the C.B.C., I was planning a broadcast. I'd like your help and cooperation.
Quebec: A dangerous word, Monsieur.

New Brunswick: All I can say is: if you plan to broadcast this story in New Brunswick then you'll have to cut out all reference to the wolf. It would be damaging to our American tourist trade.

Junior: Prince Edward Island?
P.E.I.: Yes.
Junior: I'm from the C.B.C. I want to show you a fairy tale.
P.E.I.: Ah, you mean the specifications of a tunnel to the mainland.
Junior: No, this is a fairy tale about *Little Red Riding Hood.*
P.E.I.: Foiled again. *Red Riding Hood,* eh? I'm afraid this province will not condone the girl's use of the bottle of wine.

Nova Scotia: Sorry, but ever since Bliss Carman died we have made it a point not to speak to other Canadians except when it's low tide at Grand Pre.
Junior: Oh, then you're not interested in *Little Red Riding Hood?*
Nova Scotia: Not unless her first name is *Evangeline.*

THE TORONTO Game

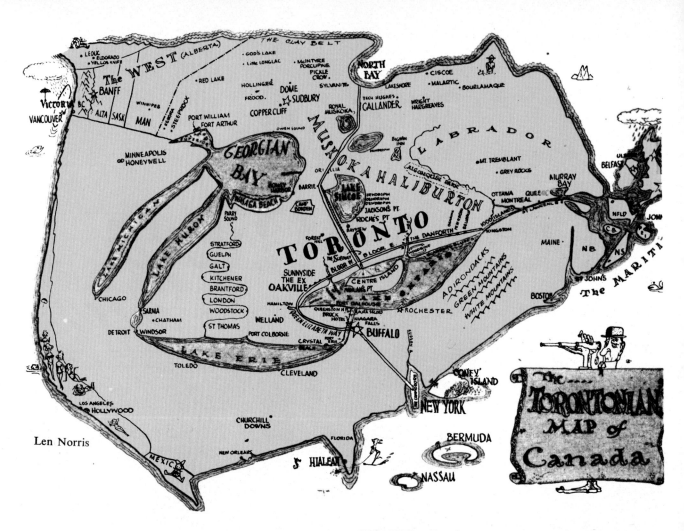

Len Norris

The TORONTONIAN MAP of Canada

First prize, one week in Toronto
Second prize, two weeks in Toronto

— *Old Canadian saying*

This sanctimonious ice box . . .

— *Wyndham Lewis*

This bush metropolis.

— *Ibid*

Compared with a Toronto Sunday, the Scottish Sabbath is a French ball.

— *Bob Edwards*

Our iron law of civic growth seems to be that the bigger Toronto gets the worse it gets.

— Toronto *Telegram*, Alexander Ross

Premier Stanfield of Nova Scotia announces his Centennial project; to try to love Toronto.

— Toronto *Star*, January 27, 1967

Hating Toronto is a custom that has added zest to the lives of thousands of Canadians. The city has a strange effect. Few people ever simply say they don't like it; they search for new and colorful ways to denounce it. At times the game has attained international scope. The bonds of shared emotions about Toronto have drawn together little groups who hate it in far-off cities like London and San Francisco. A driving desire to get out of Toronto was the theme of at least one novel. As a subject of jokes, the Queen City is gaining on Brooklyn. In its way Toronto has created a truly Canadian literature that has lost nothing from the fact that two million Torontonians continue, maddeningly, to live there.

Some of the criticisms of Toronto are based on bitter personal experience. Some are valid objective assessments of some of the things Toronto has persisted in doing to strengthen the legends about it. The columns of Richard Needham, of the Toronto *Globe and Mail,* probably don't belong in this section at all, as, in a perverse way, he seems to love the place. But the following two pieces are included because Needham has been able, with unerring, consistent skill and humour, to put his finger on some of Toronto's most ticklish spots.

Aloha, Church Street

BY RICHARD J. NEEDHAM

You have been, of course, to Tasmania, Cambodia, Siberia, and Tristan da Cunha. You have tobogganed down Mount Everest, sipped Canadian Club with Brazilian headhunters, and seen the Belfast gas works by moonlight.

What is left? How can you impress your stay-at-home friends? There is still one exotic place you haven't visited, and that is Toronto.

For the visitor, Toronto has two seasons, too hot and too cold. Whichever you choose, you will find a wide range of pageantry – the fertility rites at Don Mills, the human sacrifices on the Gardiner Expressway, the wine-tasting ceremonies in Allan Gardens, the blessing of the hockey players on the City Hall steps.

Language is no problem in Toronto; just read Chaucer and Henry Miller before you arrive. No currency difficulties; whatever kind of money you bring, the friendly merchants will knock you down to get it away from you. Driving is easy; up-to-date traffic control systems ensure that at every intersection you hit the red light.

Be admired and envied next fall, when you show your colour slides of York Township and Long Branch. Be the first in your block to have seen Toronto's lunchpail people singing and dancing as they go to work at the zipper factory. Taste the fascinating native dishes – boiled carrots, wieners and beans, fried egg sandwiches.

Explore mysterious potholes. Watch subways being built one inch at a time. Tour historic jails where people wait three months to be brought to trial. Visit University Avenue, largest mausoleum in the world.

Enjoy coffee in an all-night bistro while colourful, black-jacketed lads beat up the proprietor. Hear a Toronto cabbie give his own picturesque description of the Metro Licensing Commission. Watch Toronto City Council spend fourteen hours arguing as to who started the Crimean War.

You will never forget your vacation in this delightful, cosmopolitan city. As your ship sails away, and the sun sinks over the packinghouses, the Torontonians come streaming out of the bars to bid you farewell. Thousands of them line the shore and wave to you in their traditional style, right arm up and fist clenched. They appear a little unsteady on their feet, but they have a sure aim with a rock.

NEEDHAM BY MACPHERSON
They call him the world's oldest teenager.

Waiting for Novgorod

BY RICHARD J. NEEDHAM

If you travel 18.7 miles out of the city improper, you will come to a suburb named Hypertension Heights whose inhabitants spend most of their time on the psychiatrist's couch either because they are unhappy, or because they are happy and feel guilty about it. It was here I found myself the other night with Elaine Weeps, a white-haired little old lady who teaches Elementary Snake-charming at Boredom Sedentary here in Toronto.

The occasion was a cocktail party in honour of the famous writer, Rasputin J. Novgorod, and I was delighted when, after long delay, he showed up with one of his numerous campy aides, a poppet whom he introduced only as Mouse, and who trotted along beside him wearing a sign which read, "Men! Help this Mouse get to England! For 10 cents, a hug. For 25 cents, a kiss. For 50 cents, a telephone number which will turn out to be that of the Dominion Supermarket in Clovenhoof Mall." The sturdy little waif revealed that she went to many public gatherings with Mr. Novgorod and, by appealing to the notorious generosity of Torontonians, hoped to get enough money for as she put it, So-ho-ho-ho and away we go.

Mr. Novgorod himself cut a colourful figure with his gold-rimmed pince-nez, floor-length opera cape, and the flowing mane of white hair which has made him the bugbear of Ontario's high school vice-principals. "Just like some Celtic bard!" whispered Elaine excitedly, as we plied him with questions, compliments and triple brandies. "Is it true, sir," I asked, "that you conduct a running feud with your editor, Dietrich Doppelganger, alias Blightman?"

"Blightman speak with forked tongue," the sage replied. "When you see him approaching, you think he's wearing a Persian lamb cap. As he draws closer, you see he's bareheaded. The book which has meant most to him is Mackenzie King's *Industry and Humanity*. Everything about him is phony; even his nose, which appears to be false, is real. Blightman thinks Krafft-Ebing is one of the new cheese spreads. People dislike him on first acquaintance; when they really get to know him, their dislike turns to hatred. Slower than a speeding Newfie Bullet! Right now, he's complaining about the stockings I hung up in my office for Santa to fill. So what's wrong with them being fishnets?"

Mr. Novgorod told us of his plans for the coming year: "I am in close touch with students at such places as Rigmarole C.I., Haig and Haig Secondary, Bishop Strangle, Abject College, Applejack College, Wriggly College, Timidity College, Uppity Canada, and Allen Ginsberg Memorial. We are going to start a new political grouping here in Ontario – the Brownpaperbag Party, headed of course by the infamous Brownpaperbagman and his female accomplice, Sparkling Rosy. Our intention is to fight the 1967 provincial election on a platform of wine, women and song, not infrequently falling off it into the combo we will take around with us – Thor Veblen and His Conspicuous Wastrels."

The sage of Loathsome Mews also disclosed his scheme to start a new publication. "The name of it is *Playgirl*, the editor is Helen Heffalump, and she will expound her swinging philosophy in 187 instalments. *Playgirl* will feature exciting pictures of men without any clothes on, notably members of the House of Comics and the Senility. We will appease the Morality Squad with lavish use of, need I say, brown paper bags and liquor sales slips made out in the name of Davie Fulton. Later on there will be Playgirl Clubs, where drinks will be served by men attired as stags and wearing antlers on which the customers can stash their wigs, falls and postiches."

After his ninth triple brandy, however, Mr. Novgorod's face clouded. "It's this uneasy feeling I have about *The Archer*. It is perhaps some kind of Trojan horse? Rumor hath it that there's a secret passage underneath leading all the way down to Peking; and that at noon on July 1, 1967, millions of Chinese kulaks will come swarming out, led by the notorious warlord, Wun Hip Guy."

He lifted his tenth brandy to his lips, but suddenly there was this awful grinding noise, and he came apart like Humpty Dumpty, with pieces of metal all over the floor. Elaine started to cry and recite poetry: "Not a drum was heard, not a funeral note, as his corpse to the rampart we hurried." But Mouse hushed her up, calmly gathered the parts, and put them in a cardboard box. "It happens all the time," she said, "especially in the festering season. IBM will put him together so he's as bad as new." After she had staggered off with the box on her head, the party broke up.

Elaine and I were offered a ride back to town and accepted, though I must say that when you get 27 men and women in a Volkswagen, you're just asking for noisy silences at the breakfast table next morning. We squeezed in, however, rolled merrily along the Humbert-Lolita Freeway, and had gone all of five miles before we realized nobody was driving.

We all hate Toronto

ADAPTED FROM THE RADIO PLAY BY LISTER SINCLAIR

Once upon a time there lived a young man called Charlie. Most of the time, he was a very ordinary young man who did very ordinary things, but one day he made a dreadful decision. He called for his poor, old, leather-faced father. And he sent for his poor, old, wire-haired mother. And he told them both his dreadful decision: "I have decided to go to Toronto."

His father pleaded with him on bended knee. "Do not bring down my bald head in sorrow to the grave."

His mother said, "Force some fine old Nouveau Riche brandy, a family favourite, down my throat."

"You see, boy: you've nearly killed your mother."

"I cannot help it. The time has come to cut the apron strings."

"Here you are, an able-bodied man, respectably brought up, instead of which you decide to go to Toronto," said his father.

"My sacred principle demands it."

"What sacred principle is that?"

"Money, of course; is there any other kind?"

"Then go, my boy; when you talk like that, Toronto is undoubtedly the place for you!"

First of all, Charlie tried to find out something about this mysterious city. He asked all his friends what they thought of the place. "What do *you* all think of Toronto?"

And they answered as one man: "We all hate Toronto!"

He even took a special trip all the way to Baffin Land to conduct an informal survey among the one Eskimo he found there.

"What do *you* think about Toronto?"

"Ya ug-luk cha-chollakuk Toronto," said the Eskimo, and mark you, that was without even seeing the place!

And it was the same story everywhere. An Indian, from the remote Northwest, told Charlie the very same thing:

"How!" said Charlie. "What do *you* think of Toronto?"

"Chugh Toronto."

Which, translated, meant:

When the little Hiawatha
Took his bow and went out hunting;
Took his bow of polished birchwood,
When his feet grew hot and sweaty,
When his socks grew stiff beneath him,
He would take his socks, Wa-hee-cha,
Take his dirty socks, Wa-hee-cha;
Rinse them out in Gitchee Gumee,
Rinse them out in Big Sea Water;
And the place where once he did it,
Where he washed his socks, Wa-hee-cha,
Now the place is named Toronto,
Washing place of Hiawatha,
And ever since it's been Pa-chee-ko;
Kootch-pa-chee-ko; all washed up.

In short, everybody Charlie talked to said they hated Toronto; and in fact, doctors say that four surveys out of five prove that 98.7% of the population of Canada has given it as their considered opinion that they hate Toronto. The remaining 1.3% were

dead at the time of the survey, which had included the lounge of the Empress Hotel, Victoria, by mistake.

Why, therefore, did Charlie still want to go to Toronto?

He needed the money. You got to eat.

So Charlie set out for Toronto, the poor and despised; or rather, Toronto, the rich and despised. He knew of its wicked, wicked weather; all pure weather, never an ounce of climate; its flickering lights, the spectacle-makers' dream of heaven; and, of course, he was going there to make money. That was how he steeled himself.

"I am the captain of my soul," he said. "You got to eat."

And people never like a city they have to live in simply to make money. It may be ungrateful of them, but the curse of financial prosperity hangs over Toronto like some miasma from the low-lying swamps on which the luckless city was originally built.

Toronto, after all, is the last buttress against depression. It is the coward's castle in the famine. Depression begins at the coasts and eats its way slowly inland towards prosperous Toronto. And the rest of the country always seems a bit jealous of Toronto's relative immunity.

All these thoughts, and a great many more equally complicated, banged about in Charlie's thoughtful head, as he sat in the train on his way to Toronto, surrounded by his simple brown paper parcel. Of course, nobody else was going to Toronto; not even the most courageous.

So he came at last to Toronto, the great teeming city of eastern Canada; the swarming, seething tumultuous sky-scraper-ridden heart of Ontario! Toronto; the wealthiest city in the Dominion, its sidewalks paved with gold and obscured by an endless throng of eager, excited, happy, bustling people!

Only he happened to arrive on a Sunday.

He walked out of the huge echoing Union Station, and out into Front Street. Not a soul as far as the eye could see. Not a sound except the dust falling on the silent queue of corpses hidden away in the bowels of the Union Station still waiting for a cab. So Charlie started to walk. He trudged past the Customs and Excise Building down there by the station, bowing three times, of course, as he passed the Department of Income Tax. Then he turned up Yonge Street, stretching away straight as an arrow (and about as wide) all the way up to Hudson Bay, the Arctic Circle and North York.

So he came through the hollow empty streets of the city that nobody loves, with all the eyes of To-

ronto peeping in horror at the man who dared to walk up Yonge Street on a Sunday; till at length he came to Queen's Park, where he curled up for the night cradled in the stern bronze lap of Her Late Majesty Queen Victoria, who was not amused.

But in the morning, things had changed! It was Monday, and on Mondays, Toronto makes money! The chimneys were smoking away like a house on fire, the great column of hot air over Queen's Park announced that the legislators were pointing with pride and viewing with alarm, and, above all, crowds of people were pouring downtown with hard Toronto faces, and set Toronto jaws, all eager to make money from one another. But Charlie noticed the way they showed the whites of their teeth and flared their nostrils when they saw him lolling comfortably in the cold metal arms of Victoria the Great.

"They're all timid. They're scared I'm going to jump down and shout: 'Boo!' at them. If they weren't timid, they wouldn't notice me at all."

And Charlie settled back comfortably with his head against the good Queen's gracious shoulder and watched the people scudding past on their way to work. Presently he began to notice they all seemed to be singing a sad little song as they went spinning off to earn their money. All of them seemed to be singing it; in street cars, on bicycles, everybody seemed to be humming between his clenched Toronto teeth:

Every Monday morning
Business starts again.
Sunday's immolation
Cleansing us from sin.
Sing a song of greenbacks
Pockets full of pelf.
Out for dirty dollars
Never thought of self.
Debits and debentures;
Assets, files and dockets.
Off to put our hands in
Some one else's pockets.
Sing a song of moolah
Pockets full of scratch.
Piling up mazuma,
Watching nest-eggs hatch.
Every one is hopping
On the hunt for smackers.
Busy old Toronto,
Ain't no room for slackers.
Sing a song of money
Pockets full of dough;
Out for filthy lucre
Off to work we go!

Charlie noticed a quantity of rather disreputable characters feeding pigeons from little paper bags and themselves from little bottles. You may be sure Charlie was soon chatting away like a ton of bricks to one of these fine fellows.

"Everybody in Toronto seems to be in an awful hurry."

"They kill themselves trying to live," the man said. "What is this world if full of woes you have no time to sit and . . . doze. But you won't find any of that sort of thing in Hogtown-on-the-Don. Have some hair restorer?"

"I have lots of hair, thanks."

"Oh, well, no accounting for tastes. I regard myself as this city's last custodian of orthodox Epicureanism."

But you meet all sorts in Dollarville-on-the-Lake-shore. Present company excepted."

"Oh, yes, present company excepted."

"People here need to grumble more. Have some nail polish remover?"

"Not just this moment, thanks."

"People here need to laugh at themselves. But you can't laugh while you're looking down your long, thin aristocratic nose."

"Can't you?"

"Try it, and I'll guarantee you'll rupture an eyeball. Have some embalming fluid?"

"Not right now."

"Shoe polish?"

"No thanks."

"Oh well. The people here are all right, though. They're all right! Don't you dare say a word against them, do you hear?"

"I wouldn't dream of it!"

"Toronto is the greatest unifying influence in this country today. Without Toronto, let me tell you, this country would dissolve into the red ruin of domestic turmoil and civil war *tomorrow!* Or this afternoon even! Toronto is the one thing that holds the place together."

"But we all hate Toronto."

"That's just it. We *all* hate Toronto! It's the only thing everybody's got in common. You hear a dreadful quarrel start up between English Canadians, and French Canadians, or Maritimers and Manitobans, or some such thing. Just when they're going to cut each other's throats, somebody mentions Toronto. And what happens?"

"I don't know."

"As soon as anybody mentions Toronto, all enmity is forgotten, all scars are healed, all thoughts of violence and discord are swallowed up in warm brotherly love, and united at last in friendship, the erstwhile rival disputants can weep joyfully on one another's shoulders, as in a sublime chorus they lift up their voices in abominable vilification of Toronto, the Queen City! Long may she continue to rot!

And that's how Charlie came to live in Toronto, the city we all hate. Of course, there are people who say a city with so many museums and theatres and art galleries and orchestras – there are people who say that such a city cannot be wholly bad. But these people invariably turn out to be Torontonians.

And, by the way, Charlie is a Torontonian now. He settled down there eventually. Yes, he changed his name to John A. Macdonald, and settled down, and, like the hundreds of thousands of other people, lived in Toronto happily ever after!

"...the part **I** can't understand is how he can **honestly** go on watching the hockey games..."

BARRON
TORONTO STAR

Sid Barron spoofed the Toronto scene for the Toronto Star – even after he settled in Alberta.
'I never hated Toronto," Barron says, "I just figured it wasn't worth the effort."

In 1964 McKenzie Porter, an English journalist with a spell-binding vocabulary, who had written for *Maclean's* for many years, began writing a daily column for the Toronto *Telegram*. Probably no writer, before or since, has given Torontonians such a skilful needling. Today there are still Toronto businessmen who sit quietly cursing Porter and vowing that they will wear white shirts to the office till the day they die because of an early column he wrote in which he said that the local practice of wearing a white shirt downtown in the daytime was in unforgivably bad taste, and made the wearers look like bicycle salesmen.

Snobbery, like anger, is a very delicate instrument of humour. It has to be used just the right way or it becomes dull. Some journalistic snobs give the feeling of a real underlying, complacent snobbery which provides humour with nothing to bounce on. McKenzie Porter, on the other hand, gives the feeling of being a tentative, nervous, high-strung snob with underlying self doubts, which makes all the difference. When Porter refers to his Toronto readers as forelock-tugging serfs, or says when he travels by air he is "dispirited by the dulcet voice of an invisible female who welcomes me aboard and presumes that I am avid to know the names of the driver and the maids," I get the feeling that a fine nervous tremor passes through his fingers as they rest on his typewriter, that he is really facing the mob and giving as good as he gets, and that in black moments he would be quite capable of writing about himself with equal derision. The following column written on his return from a trip to India gives (eventually) his impressions of watching Torontonians eat ice cream cones.

But hush! What manner of man is this who comes lurching out of the sunset, a gaunt crooked figure uttering little animal cries and occasional shouts of maniacal laughter!

A Retainer: Is it Gyascutus, the Human Bat of Avignon?

Myself: No, no, no, you rustic dunce.

Retainer: Could it be Dipas the Athenian Necrophile?

Myself: Of course it is not, you unlettered lumpkin.

Retainer: Then it must be Prock, the Moving Corpse of Samarkand.

Myself: You illiterate bondsman! You inarticulate scullion! You retarded vassal! Have you no eyes?

It is I. *C'est moi*. It is McKenzie Porter himself, the Marco Polo of Toronto, the unsung Shelley of the 20th century, returning to work.

Retainer: Where have you been?

Myself: I have been for two weeks' holiday in New York, London, Paris, Frankfurt, Rome, Beirut, Bombay, Delhi, Kashmir, Moscow, Manchester, Blackpool, Oswaldtwistle, Giggleswicken and East Gwillimbury, Ontario.

Retainer: And what did you do in East Gwillimbury?

Myself: I built a monument, eight-feet high out of three tons of rock left over from a field-stone fireplace.

Retainer: To whom did you build this monument?

Myself: You cringing lickspittle! You forelock tugging serf! You kneeling thrall! To whom do you think! I built it to myself. Any man who endures such a holiday deserves a monument. Indeed I shall never forgive Torontonians for not building in my honour at least a pyramid...

On my return from India, which is in some ways the richest but in most ways the poorest country in the world, it is understandable that I received some sharp new impressions of Toronto.

The spectacle which hit me most forcefully on a sunny Sunday afternoon was that of the enormous number of adults who were engaged as ruminatively as any cud-chewing cow, in the operation of licking ice cream cones.

The blank-eyed abstraction in which grown men and women apply themselves to this form of infantile refreshment is vibrant with Freudian overtones.

I cannot think of any other country on earth, save the United States, wherein mature citizens eat on the streets with such indelicacy.

While it is most unhygienic it is at least tolerable to see toddlers sucking ice cream cones in city atmospheres packed with suspended microbial muck. But the sight of their mothers and fathers slurping and slavering in public over these chilly hemispheres of vegetable fat, sugar and powdered milk is more than I can stomach.

Surely it is possible for most of us in this, the second richest country of all, to eat ice cream out of a cardboard carton, indoors, with a cardboard spoon. There is, of course, only one civilized way in which to eat ice cream and that is from a crystal goblet with a small spoon fashioned out of ivory.

THE SPORTS ARENA

There's no logical reason why sports writers should be humorists, but they frequently are. Ted Reeve of the Toronto *Telegram* not only wrote funny columns but became the subject of many stories told around the press clubs. He had a quick wit. Asked, one time in the locker room when he was with a lacrosse team: "What's the crowd like out there, Ted?" he retorted "Happy as hell. He just lit a cigar." Reeve was reputed to be one of the most frightening looking soldiers ever to enlist in the Canadian Army, a tall, gaunt, raffish man with a nose that made good publicity shots whenever Jimmy Durante was in Toronto, and he was the only man, according to eye witnesses, who could make a beret look rumpled. One time an officer said, "Reeve, there's a man here who says he's a friend of yours." "The man's an impostor," snapped Reeve.

The most indecipherable of all writing is sports writing. Normally, no one except an avid fan and. dedicated sports column reader can figure out what the writer is talking about. Reeve himself writes at times like someone from outer space: it's literally impossible for a non-sports-fan to make out what game was played, let alone who won. Yet Reeve is an extremely well-read man who smuggles more culture and intellect into the sports pages than any Canadian writer, without most of his readers even suspecting it, even bringing in Keat's *Ode to a Grecian Urn*, and explaining its meaning very deftly. He also wrote abominable verse himself, signing his works Alice Snippersnapper and Moaner McGruffey.

CHRISTMAS CAROL
BY TED REEVE

It was Christmas Eve, very clear and very still except that way off in the distance bells were ringing, the fireplace was burning low, and everyone had gone to bed except our old friend Nutsy Fagan and his favourite nephew, who he called Little Joe because he was four. Little Joe was not in bed because he had been looking forward to the visit of one Mr. Claus

I'll stay right where I am
BY MOANER McGRUFFEY

On California's sun-kissed slopes
    the rose-run bowers bloom,
And colonnades of colour rise
    to where the mountains loom;
The orange groves line the wide white roads
    where cars come floating by
With beauties out of Hollywood
    that ease the weary eye.
When blizzards blow I often long
    for California's calm,
But they lack big league hockey, so
    I'll stay right where I am.

The blue Pacific's lapping
    on the far-off coral strand
Of a fair Marquesan Island
    with its stretching golden sand;
Where all is gay profusion
    and the strumming natives play

Their sad and rhythmic music
    as the palms and maidens sway.
We would sail into that haven
    as the tropic moon came up
If it wasn't that by doing it
    we would miss the Stanley Cup.

In the white-walled Estraleda
    as it hangs above the sea
The sun-splashed old piazzas have
    a strange appeal for me;
The silken haze of summer seems to
    cling along that shore,
And out around the deep blue sky
    the snow-white sea birds soar.
Oh, I would love to wander to
    • that land of blue lagoons
If it were not for the visits of
    the Montreal Maroons.

for so long that he got himself all wound up like a top, only more so, and like a lot of other young gentlemen of that age, on that very special night, he was quite full of the old agog.

So that is why he was on hand to remark: "Uncle Nutsy, why do you take so long to look through those Christmas cards?" To which Uncle Nutsy replied: "Well, Little Joseph, on these cards I meet a great many of my old friends that I have been meeting every Christmas since I was knee high to a duck, and it makes me feel very glad to meet them all again. Like, for instance, the coachman on this card, who has been driving that good old stage coach across Christmas cards ever since he retired from driving it across the English countryside.

"That, in fact," continued Uncle Nutsy, "is the very Muggleton coach in which Mr. Pickwick rode down to Wardles for Christmas, well wrapped up in shawls, great coats and comforters. There is the very guard who put the oyster barrels and the codfish into the boot and the hot brandy and water into himself in the company of Samuel Weller. The very guard who blew the lively tune on the key bugle on the cold, clear air as the coach skimmed over the hard frosty ground and then rattled through the paved streets of a country town. And a very mean bugle he blows, too, and later on tonight if we sit here very quiet we may hear it."

"Are these old friends of ours also, Uncle Nutsy?" said Joseph, handing up a picture of four assorted Christmas waifs, holding forth outside a large though rickety looking castle.

"They are, indeed," said Uncle Nutsy, "and I can tell that they are doing their very best, just by the slant of their heads. Some people now, Joe, would not know whether those lads were rendering *One Christmas Morn a Merry King* or *Minnie Had a Heart as Big as a Whale*. But I know them. Reading from left to right, they are Simpkin, Samkin, Watkin and Peterkin. In fact, they are all kin, and right here they are just reaching the top register of the *Wenceslaus* suite, which is why the toes of their shoes are turning up that way. Simkin, in the green jerkin, is the one playing the dulcimer, while Samkin is blowing his soul into that fish horn. There used to be a curve in it, but he blew it out playing flats. Watkin is the

How Lou Skuce saw his colleague Ted Reeve (or "Moaner McGruffey," take your pick) at his desk.

short stout one who goes after the high notes, and Peterkin is the long gent who dives for the low notes, as life is like that. And when Peterkin really has to go to his deepest he disappears right inside that collar and comes up, a few moments later, with the necessary chunk of profundo. Why, look now, how that castle is swaying to their harmony."

"Who lives in that castle, Uncle Nutsy?" says Little Joe, and Uncle Nutsy says, "Why nobody but a happy old guy called Sir Montagu-Montagu-Montagu, who they call Monty-Monty-Monty for short, and judging by the lights in all the windows, they are having a real Old Yuletide gathering as usual. The men-at-arms will be putting on the Yule log, and the steward will be adding a couple more vats to the wassail bowl just to get the right mixture.

"It was on such a night as this that Sir Montagu's brother, Sir Barnaby, became the original Christmas Ghost. They were doing a little jousting on the drawbridge to work up an appetite, and someone hit him on the helmet with a snowball. It had snowed hard that day, and whoever tossed the snowball had plenty on his fast one, for Sir Barnaby straightaway left this vale of cheers on horseback.

89

"He turns up every Christmas, however, at some of the oldest homes in England, and is very popular, as he is the only ghost that works on horseback. The 'Galloping Ghost' they call him, and as they don't know exactly where he will turn up next, the best families always fill a jar with smoke from the fire and leave it for Sir Barnaby, who generally leaves the jar for a refill, but takes the smoke and wears it for a muffler or a blanket for his horse."

Little Joe was starting to nod by now, but he was a game one, and he came up with one more card. It was a picture of an old inn yard, into which another coach was coming, and the rosy old innkeeper and the help are all ahustle and abustle, and in the foreground are two little boys in snuff-colored vests and big caps that looked as though they might get the best of them at any moment. They were waiting there with green suitcases, evidently on their way home for the holidays.

"Those two little boys," said Uncle Nutsy, "have been waiting for that coach for a long time now, but they are still looking forward to it. You can see they are feeling pretty good, for their last night at school they had a hamper from Auntie Agatha and they sat up in the dormitory with candles and they and their fellow-students knocked off a lot of jelly and seed cake and had a very merry time in a quiet way until a prefect came around. But that didn't matter so near Holiday time, and here they are on their way to the Manor, and no matter how long they wait for that coach to get around the corner, they are still having much the best of it, for they have so much to look forward to.

"And that, Little Joe, is the secret of success in this now life, for if you ever get so you lose the knack of having something to look forward to, you are beat, no matter what your bank book may say. Like the people on the Grecian Urn that poor Mr. Keats wrote about, those two little boys in the Inn Yard are not getting anywhere fast, but they are still full of that feeling that the best is yet to come. So . . ."

But Little Joe was dozing now, so Uncle Nutsy carried him up to bed, and when he said good-night he said: "You will never be a Tiny Tim, Little Joe, because by the feel of your young legs you will grow up instead to be a middle wing or a second defence half-back, but nevertheless tell Uncle Nutsy what it was that Tiny Tim said."

"God Bless Us One and All, said Tiny Tim," said Little Joe.

"That," said Uncle Nutsy, "is the right answer."

Jack Reppen's Sports Types

Reppen, a fine artist of great promise, turned out amusing sports caricatures as a profitable sideline.

Speakest thou Sportuguese?

BY MAGGIE GRANT

It takes all kinds of writers to make up a newspaper and I sometimes wonder if those who compose their messages in Spanish, French or other languages have diverged and developed along such devious lines as we who write in English. Take sports writers, now. To my mind they use a jargon almost incomprehensible to all but those who have followed sports pages from birth. Yet from time to time one or another of these scribes has been heard to say, in manner most lofty, "Of course, I never read the women's pages."

At this point women writers are supposed to rush forward and pin a medal on the fellow, I suppose, but I've been rather more inclined to snarl: "Because, undoubtedly, you've arrived at the point where you no longer understand plain English."

The trouble with sports news is there's such an awful lot of it that items are continually spilling over onto other pages, catching a reader unawares. By way of example I offer this, which I happened upon some months ago, sandwiched into the legal notices:

ROCKETS EDGE HOLLAND MARSH

Now, a veteran sports fan would undoubtedly realize that this signified the defeat of one hockey team by another hockey team. But to such as I, it spelt inter-continental ballistic missiles. "Why the Holland Marsh?" I kept asking myself as I fumbled for my glasses.

This little misapprehension on my part set me to wondering what will happen to me when I can no longer read anything but the large type. Simply imagine what is printed beneath, I suppose. And as a sort of test run I leafed through a stack of old sports pages, selecting a few headings, and then thought of stories to fit them. Several follow:

BALL OF FIRE BURNS UP EAST YORK TRACK
(Toronto *Telegram*)

Citizens of East York were thrown into a panic yesterday when a giant ball of fire appeared over the township and plunged on to a spur line of the Canadian Pacific Railway. The rails were turned to molten metal. Contacted later by the *Tely,* Dunlap Observatory refused to comment.

PACKER BACK FACES CHARGES
(Hamilton *Spectator*)

Pflloyde Smith, a packing plant employee, yesterday turned aside a stampede of wild heifers consigned for slaughter by facing them with his back. "This is, by all odds, the most effective method in a case of this sort and I heartily recommend it to persons wishing to follow the career of my choosing," Mr. Smith shouted to interested spectators as the herd thundered past.

RIDERS USE STAMPS TO CATCH CATS
(Toronto *Telegram*)

A near riot was averted in Maple Leaf Gardens during last night's performance of the Canadian Championship Rodeo when a pride of alley cats stampeded into the ring. Leaping to their saddles, cowboys and cowgirls put on a dazzling display of horsemanship to save the day. Licking pinky stamps at full gallop, they scooped up the cats by sticking the stamps to their fur.

WALKER PACES WINDSOR
(Toronto *Star*)

During the past week a mysterious stranger wearing a toga and bedroom slippers has been observed pacing the streets of Windsor. Yesterday our reporter obtained an interview with the man, who identified himself as Hobart Arf, 92, a professional walker. Mr. Arf's leisure-time hobby is pacing off the cities of Canada. He announced that Toronto can expect him early in July.

Nanoodnik Of The North

BY JIM COLEMAN

Nanoodnik Of The North was born far out on the barren tundra and she was typically Canadian. That is to say that she was a mixture of Cree, Irish, French, English and Esquimaux and her high cheekbones and her sallow complexion hinted at an influx of blood from the mysterious and exotic Far East.

Nanoodnik Of The North grew up in a very, very small town. In fact, it would be stretching a point to call it a town; it would be more accurate to describe it as a widening on the ice pack.

Nanoodnik Of The North had a typically Canadian childhood in that she complained about lumps in her breakfast bowl of blubber and she demanded ketchup on her pemmican. But she was a Good Canadian and she grew up to be the strongest girl in our history. When she was only 6, she was beating 12-year-old boys at such neighborhood games as Indian-wrestling, leap-the-crevasse and snap-the-walrus.

It was Pierre Radisson, an importunate travelling salesman from Montreal, who persuaded Nanoodnik Of The North to represent Canada in the Olympic Games. Radisson, who was huckstering mass-produced harpoons among the seal and walrus-hunters, stayed overnight with Nanoodnik's family. Nanoodnik's mother ran out of sugar and she asked Nanoodnik to borrow a cup of sugar from "the lady next door."

Now, it happened that "the-lady-next-door" lived 12 miles away. Nanoodnik made the 24-mile run in three hours and seven minutes.

Radisson, who, out of idle curiosity, had been timing her on his vest-pocket lumpy, almost fell out of his moose-antler chair in surprise when Nanoodnik scampered in with the cup of sugar. Talking swiftly, he convinced the parents that Nanoodnik could bring Honor to Canada by running at the Olympic Games in Athens. The parents assented readily, since they had 22 other children.

Pierre Radisson arrived in Montreal with Nanoodnik Of The North in the spring of the following year. He arranged with his firm to sponsor her trip to Greece. In the meantime, she ate him out of house and home (blubber was as expensive as caviar in Montreal). So, one day, Radisson heard that St. Jacques Societé was sponsoring a sports meet with a prize of $500 for the Marathon.

Radisson entered Nanoodnik Of The North in the Marathon, although girls weren't permitted to compete in track meets in those days. No one realized that Nanoodnik was a girl because she wore long sealskin pants and a sealskin parka which successfully disguised all the customary bumps and curves which are believed to distinguish girls from boys.

Nanoodnik Of The North won the Montreal Marathon by two miles and she was photographed receiving a cheque for $500 from the Mayor of Montreal. (Dr. Percy Moore, historian for the Department of Northern Affairs, says his researches convince him that Nanoodnik received none of the money – Radisson cashed the cheque.)

The record books reveal that the Marathon at the 1900 Olympic Games in Athens was won by Teato, of France, in the time of two hours and 59 minutes.

Two nights before the Marathon, Radisson had given Nanoodnik a secret workout. The great Canadian athlete had covered the Marathon distance in two hours and 38 minutes. She was so exhilarated after her run that she scaled the locked gate of the Athens Zoo and she played snap-the-inmates for an hour or so.

On the afternoon of the Marathon, there was great excitement when Canada's mysterious entry appeared at the starting-line. Nanoodnik was wearing her long sealskin pants and her sealskin parka with the word "Canada" emblazoned across her chest in red letters.

Then, it happened. Just as the starter was calling the competitors to the mark, a Russian official rushed on the scene, gesticulating and waving a newspaper clipping. There was a 20-minute delay while the official interpreters translated into four languages.

Olympic officials examined the newspaper clipping in horror. The Russians had produced a copy of the Montreal paper which showed Nanoodnik receiving that cheque for $500. Nanoodnik was led weeping from the Olympic Stadium; disqualified for being a professional runner.

And that is the story of how Canada was deprived of a certain victory in the Marathon at the 1900 Olympic Games in Athens.

And, that is just another example of the stinking, rotten type of officiating which Canadian teams meet in international sports competitions. Hurrah for the Canadians! To hell with the Russians!

Okay, boys and girls – let's go out on the field and beat the ... out of them! Let's win this one for Nanoodnik Of The North!

Home
&
Family

I know I'm going to hear about including two of my own pieces here and I'll give my reasons now and hope it's the last I hear of it. (a) When I mentioned that I was editing a book of Canadian humour to an editor for whom I've written what I thought was humour for many years, he looked at me sourly across his desk and said, "You wrote something that made me laugh once. It was about ten years ago – something about a school"; (b) they are very short; (c) I've probably written as much about children and family life as any other Canadian writer.

Children are monsters

Whenever I tell my friends that I write at home, they imply that I'm lucky to be able to work in peace and quiet, completely free of distractions.

Actually, each morning as I sit with my fingers poised over my typewriter looking out onto a deceptively quiet street I find myself the lone spectator of a nether world of mayhem, treachery and propaganda that often keeps me absorbed for hours.

As each man leaves the house for downtown, pre-school-age children are turned outdoors, one by one, their little faces wiped clean of toast crumbs and their souls full of diabolical plans. They pass my window all day long, in thin-column formation, in a perpetual state of spine-chilling, dead-pan, passionless war. They wear hunting caps, long pink nightgowns, their mothers' shoes and lace curtains. Sometimes they move by on wheels, sometimes on foot, but they all have one objective; to frame one another.

By lunchtime, things have become so snarled that it's impossible to tell who is telling the truth. Right and wrong are so balled up in one gumbo mixture of bubble gum and tricycles that none of the mothers could sort them out, even if they wanted to. They just don't worry about it.

The other day I watched two little boys with shaved heads ride around a tree on their tricycles, slowly and aimlessly, from eight in the morning till suppertime, telling one another in agitated voices that they'd break one another's tricycles, that they'd climb up onto lamp posts and drop rocks on one another's heads, that they'd put one another in jail. Around eleven o'clock, one of them got off his trike, went over and hit the other in the mouth, then went home hollering, "Mummy! Pete hit me."

His mother came out, looked at him sharply, said, "Pull your pants up," and went back in.

Two strange little boys meeting for the first time will stand looking into one another's faces for a moment, then start conscientiously kicking one another until one starts howling and goes home.

Little tots with legs like noodles toddle off each morning in pigtails, bows, pocket-size dresses, on their way to play a day-long game, the object of which is to try to get somebody else spanked. When they score, they all stand around sucking their popsicles watching. They don't laugh or gloat or show any excitement. Their faces are completely expressionless.

Every other minute they go and tell their mothers. If they haven't anything to tell them, they tell them anything. Sometimes they tell their own mothers, sometimes they tell the other kid's mother. If they can't find either mother they tell the breadman. It's a peculiar world where the idea seems to be if you can stay with it until everyone is grown up it will all sort itself out.

The other day a little girl with a head of white curls let out a nerve-shattering scream that brought six mothers racing from their doors, three of them in curlers.

"Doris! What *is* it!" gasped one of them.

Doris put her hand on her flat little chest, looked across a geranium hedge at another little girl, and said in a hoarse stage whisper, "Gail looked at me!"

"It's time you came in for lunch anyway," her mother said.

One afternoon three little girls were playing. Suddenly two of them pushed the third off the veranda, then picked up her doll and threw it at her, breaking its head. I was almost ready to leap up from my typewriter and cross the road to lecture them on the rudiments of justice, sportsmanship and the Geneva Conference. The little girl who had been shoved off the veranda screamed. The other two screamed back at her. The woman of the house came out.

"They broke my doll's head," the little girl wailed.

"Why did you break Susan's doll?" the woman asked, mechanically retying a bow.

"We were through playing with her," one said.

"Pull up your socks," the woman said, "and don't get dirty."

One time I listened to one youngster ask in a flat monotone, at intervals all morning, if the other would let her play with her doll carriage.

"Can I have your carriage?" she'd say.

"No."

At noon the mother of the kid with the carriage put her head out the door and called her daughter in for lunch. The youngster put the top of the carriage up and started for home, and fell down the veranda steps. She lay on her back, reaching for a sound proportionate to the fall. I could hear the scream coming like water working its way up to the nozzle of a garden hose. Just before it arrived the other kid who stood looking down at her like a little Richard Widmark in pigtails, evidently figuring that she was going to die, said, "Can I have your carriage now?"

Mercy seems something that begins to show itself around voting age. My own youngest daughter who, although going to school, is still young enough to retain the preschool spirit, will chatter away at lunch.

"There's a boy in our class named Johnny," she'll say, industriously spooning chicken-noodle soup into herself. "He talks all the time."

"M – hm," I say.

"This morning the teacher said, 'Well I'm going to put you between two good little girls, Martha and Mary'." (Mary is my daughter.)

"So?" I say.

"'And if you talk', she said, 'I'm going to ask Martha and Mary to tell me and I'm going to send you to the office.' We had great fun."

"How do you mean?"

"We tried to get him to talk so we could tell the teacher."

"You *what*!" I bring her into focus. It's just beginning to dawn on me what she said.

"We tried to see how we could get him to talk," she says, getting up to get some more soup.

My wife says, "Oh, Mary, you shouldn't!"

"Shouldn't what?" Mary says, in surprise.

"Shouldn't take more soup," my wife says.

In the world of women and children, promises and systems of ethics are held together lightly by a thin coating of orange juice and hair fix and an occasional safety pin. It often leaves me wishing that I were back downtown amid the jolly cut-throat atmosphere of big business. There, people do one another in according to firm principles. Back home, nobody would recognize a principle if they found it in their shredded wheat.

It amounts to the same thing, probably, but it's easier on the nerves when it doesn't take place on a quiet sunny street.

SUMMER'S END

BY MARY LOWREY ROSS

Falling leaf and fading tree
And the city calls to the family.
Now autumn summer's pleasure cancels –
– Do you really need that bag of clamshells?
They're rather smelly, dear, and muddy.
Teacher wants them for Nature Study.
All right then, we'll let Teacher worry,
So put them in the trunk. But hurry,
We have to be home in time for supper.
No, dear, you'll have to wear your upper,
And you can't go barefoot. Get your sandals.
Bathing suits go on the car-door-handles.
I don't know *where* the bicycles go,
Someone can sit on the radio.

Darling, your garter-snake is pretty
But you know she'll *hate* it in the City.
Besides I really can't undertake
To share the bath with a garter-snake.
Just let her go. No one will steal her.
All *right* then. Put her in the sealer.

But if I find her in the cream
She'll have to go to the Museum.
Let's see now, mice seed, insect sugar,
– A *sealer*! Not the pressure cooker! –
Termite powder for each post
And chloride of lime where it's needed most.
And for every visiting woodland denizen
DDT as a parting benison.

I said your upper. Please put it on,
Now where on earth is Felicia gone?
She saw us packing for the City –
Here, kitty, kitty, kitty!
Look in the woodpile. Search the shore,
Maybe she's under the cabin floor.
She heard us planning to leave today
And just deliberately sneaked away.
Oh, there's nothing worse to take on vacations
Than cats that listen to conversations.
Maybe we'd better just unpack
And coax her into coming back.

How often do I have to speak?
Those turtles go back in the creek.
We'll hardly need this box of gravel.
Darling, a hornet's nest won't travel.
That mud-cat's looking rather sick.
Look! There's Felicia. Catch her quick!
Here comes Felicia, yowling and snarling,

Why I hate my kid's teacher

BY ROBERT THOMAS ALLEN

I used to draw insulting pictures of the teacher when I was a boy. I still do, only now it's my kid's teacher, a big gangling six-foot farmer's son named Wire, from a place called Appleton. Instead of drawing them on the blackboard, I draw them on place mats and cardboard coasters. I pretend I'm throwing spitballs at him and putting thumbtacks on his chair. He sits in the schoolroom doing the same thing to me and dreaming up things to drive me nuts.

One favourite trick of his is to wait till my kid wears a new dress to school, then think up what he calls a "project." This consists of making little model farms, with cows and everything, with a mixture he makes himself out of melted crayons, chalk, berry juice and mucilage. My kid comes in the door stained from head to foot and says casually:

"Mr. Wire gave us a project today."

My wife takes one look at her, turns to me and tells me that I can fork over five dollars for a new dress. She knows from experience that this stuff Wire whips up is a permanent dye that digs in like a tattoo. My wife has tried everything on it, including nail-polish remover, and it won't move. I've seen six mothers all come out onto their porches after one of these projects, holding up frocks to one another, then all turn like pioneer mothers gazing toward Pawnee country and look toward the school, where Wire is sitting dreaming up the next day's project.

Careful. Don't let her claw you, darling.
Has anyone seen the mercurochrome?
– No, you can't take that land-crab home.
I'm sorry to seem to lose my patience,
But I just won't travel with live crustaceans.
Here, zip her into the duffle-bag,
And wrap your finger in a rag.
(I warned you, darling, when you took
Those bandaids for your snapshot book.)

We're off at last. No turning back
For anything we forgot to pack.
The empty cans from our summer's stay
Go jingle, jingle, all the way.
Past the beach where last vacationists cling
To a season already on the wing,
The babies still with summer glowing
And Grandma with her midriff showing.
Past the thinning wood that meets the shore
And the sleepy barns, and the dreaming store
Where the rural grocer with simple guile
Blends city prices with country style.

Look, there's a sight to feast your eyes on –
A field of corn that meets the horizon,
(The owner of which will gladly barter
Three ears for one deflated quarter.)
Now fast recedes both wood and shore –
Did anyone close the Little House door?

The fields spread wide with autumn clover
And the popsicle spreads on the new seat cover.
Who cares?

Free at last from crisis and action,
We rest in beautiful stupefaction.
Summer is over . . . What is it, dear?
No, Felix isn't behaving queer,
He's only restless and tired, poor pup!
Quick, stop the car, he's just thrown up!
Don't scream. Watch Felix. Watch Felicia.
Now where's that box of cleansing tissue?
All right now. Everybody out.
Nothing to make a fuss about.
We'll clean it up and then we'll spread
The morning paper that nobody's read.
Isn't it fun? Who'd want to skip
The jolliest part of the whole damn trip?
Of course, it's bound to leave a stain –
Now, everybody in again.

We're nearly home. Thank heaven for that.
The children doze. The dog and cat
Forget their common enmity
In shared adjacent misery.
What is that signal flashing bright?
Darlings! It's a traffic light!
Oh, isn't it wonderful, isn't it splendid
To think our vacation's really ended!

"We're going to make coloured birds out of pieces of soap tomorrow," my kid says happily. "Mr. Wire says to ask you for some fountain-pen ink, cocoa, a can of No. 20 motor oil and your electric razor."

All the time I'm being asked by editorials to sympathize with the poor underpaid teacher, I picture this guy sitting at his desk, while his class scratches away busily, dozing over some book like *Adventures in Punctuation* and thinking up new ways to irritate me. Sometimes he does it with casual little remarks.

My kid won't believe anything I tell her, but Wire could tell her that the sun was four inches wide and made out of old light bulbs and she'd include it among the facts of nature. I don't mind it when he sticks to remarks about school work, but sometimes he evidently just says anything that comes into his mind. The last thing he told my kid was that little girls should never sleep in after six in the morning as it was bad for their spines. The result was that my youngster was up at about five-thirty, getting in my way while I tried to make my breakfast and asking me things like how you go about getting pregnant, before I'd even had my coffee.

One time he arranged for me to take charge of six kids at a school outing to a pioneer museum in a town 20 miles away, then made me responsible for my group turning in a report, with the result that before the day was over I was walking on my ankles, trying to get the answers to: (a) name eight instruments used by blacksmiths; (b) how did the early Virginians deliver mail; (c) draw a diagram of the museum; (d) name six countries where you find owls. That night the outing was followed by a school concert and I saw Wire sitting behind a fat, scowling little boy who was blowing a trumpet, grinning at me and eating my wife's fudge.

My kid thinks everything Wire says is funny. His humour is relayed to me at the supper table. It leaves me helping myself to more creamed peas, but the kids think he's a riot.

97

"Gee, Mr. Wire was funny today," my kid says. "He's the *craziest* man. Today he said – " her voice goes taut and wavers with mirth. "He said, 'I'm thirsty,' and went to the fountain and had a drink of water. Honest, the whole class nearly rolled on the floor."

I wait to hear what Wire said when he lifted his head from the fountain. Maybe he let the water drip from his chin, pretended he was a buffalo surprised at a water hole and stomped up and down the aisles. But my kid just starts helping herself to more potatoes. Evidently the joke is over. What Wire did that put the kids in the aisles was to say he was thirsty. He must get his gags out of a seed catalogue, but he panics the kids.

The maddening part of all this is that my kid dotes on this yokel Wire and thinks I'm a bum, and Wire knows it. One sunny morning last spring I came downstairs feeling especially good, tossed off my tomato juice and said to my kid, "Well, waddaya say we play hooky today?"

"Play what?" she asked.

"Play hooky," I said. "We can smoke stink worts and spear frogs."

She looked at her mother and back to me as if I'd gone nuts. "What's it mean?" she said.

"What's it *mean*?" I yelped. I turned to my wife. "Look, f'r . . . what are they teaching kids today when they don't even know what playing hooky means?" I turned back to my kid, "It means staying away from school."

"Why should I stay away from school?"

I was beginning to feel irresponsible, an unfit father·for a well-adjusted child and a bit like an old juvenile delinquent.

"You mean you don't want to stay away from school?" I said.

"Why should I stay away from school? Today we have a movie, play tennis, correct our teacher's mistakes, have phiz ed, home ec, group co-operation, square dancing, play basketball and write a report for Mr. Wire on all the things we don't like about parents."

I began to feel exactly the way I used to when I was on my way to the principal's office, peered at by clean, neat little girls in middies who took a couple of steps sideways to let me pass. In fact I began to feel maladjusted, and I give Wire fair warning he'd better not invite me to any parents' nights this year or it's going to end up with me having a temper tantrum and going around rubbing things off his blackboard and upsetting a few paper baskets.

Laughing with GARY LAUTENS

NEW YORK:

Wives have a way of getting down to basics very quickly.

"How much money do you have?" mine asked me even before we cleared the train station on our way here.

"Why?" I exclaimed.

"I just want to know."

"How much do you have?" I countered.

"Four dollars," she said.

"I have about $200."

"Good," she replied. "That's $102 each."

It seems I am fated to spend my life with women who are short on cash and long on division.

"There isn't much room in these things," I commented, trying to take off my coat in our compartment. Just then the train lurched and (I confess it) I had to grab hold of my wife for support.

"Watch it," she warned. "Get your hands off me. Where do you think you are – at the office?"

I apologized. "Shunting, I expect."

Fortunately the customs inspector came along.

"Business or pleasure trip?" he asked.

I admitted I still wasn't sure. He seemed to understand and left without touching our luggage.

My wife was disappointed. "We could be smugglers," she explained. "What's the point of being honest if you're not searched?"

I didn't argue the point.

"This is the first time I've ever been in a railway sleeper," she said – and proceeded to flick all the switches, turn all the dials and push all the buttons.

"I don't think you should have stepped on that treadle, not while we're still in the station," I said.

"I thought it was a light switch you could work

with your foot if your hands were soapy," she said.

Eventually we got to bed; I got the upper.

"Put something against the door," my wife requested.

I climbed down, propped a suitcase.

"Can you show me how to turn off the fan?" she asked.

I climbed down, turned off the fan.

"You forgot to kiss me goodnight," she said.

I climbed down, kissed her.

"You're puffing," she noticed. "You should learn to relax."

I promised I would.

The next morning we got to New York.

"Let's go to the Bronx Zoo or for a walk down Broadway or to Rockefeller Center to see the ice-skaters or . . ."

"Let's go to Macy's or Gimbel's," she interrupted.

"Central Park is lovely this time of year."

"It's too dangerous."

"Muggers don't operate in the daylight," I protested.

"I don't mean muggers – pigeons," she said.

"It's supposed to be lucky . . ."

"They're killing all kinds of people. I read it in the papers. Let's go shopping."

We compromised and had breakfast – at Rumpelmayer's, a restaurant famous for its French cooking.

"What will you have foist?" the waitress asked.

We settled for French toast with wild mountain blackberry syrup – $3.15 for a double order.

"Let's go for a walk now," I suggested.

We were doing very well, enjoying free air and sunshine, looking at the happy faces of motorists flipping for jaywalkers.

"I'd like to go to the washroom," my wife announced.

"But where . . ."

"We'll find one. I bet there's one in that big store over there. What's it called? S-A-K-S."

"We're only twelve blocks from the hotel," I protested.

The ladies' washroom at Saks is located on the fourth floor, near lingerie and shoes.

"Nice negligee. Only $300," my wife said.

"I thought you wanted to go to the washroom."

"Isn't that a cute vest – $50. And that brassiere! Just $35."

"Don't talk like that," I whispered.

"Brassiere is a perfectly good word. We're married."

"I didn't mean that. I was talking about the $35."

Finally we left Saks.

"Eaton's is better," she said firmly.

"More style, better prices, friendlier . . ."

"I was talking about the washrooms," she corrected.

Actually we escaped with only one purchase – two corkscrews. I was told they'd make lovely Christmas gifts.

We had lunch down in Greenwich Village at a small intimate place.

"Look," my wife said in a low voice. "See that young man over there – the one with the violin case. I think he's a member of Cosa Nostra."

"Why do you think that?"

"He just leaned over and kissed the other fellow at the table on the cheek."

The evidence seemed irrefutable. We quickly finished lunch and fled.

"Let's get away from the usual tourist haunts," I suggested.

"Where do you want to go?"

"Radio City Music Hall," I replied. "The movie V.I.P. is playing. Liz Taylor plays the part of a woman who had been married to this man for thirteen years . . ."

"Obviously a fantasy," my wife commented.

Anyway it was worth $1.29 to get her off the street and away from the shops.

After dinner in one of those chain steak houses ($1.19 for charcoal broiled steak, potato salad and garlic toast), we went back to the hotel.

"We've been gone almost 24 hours now," my wife said. "Isn't it wonderful to be on your own."

"Yes," I said.

"Let's call home," she suggested.

"Good idea. Poor little kids will be lonely."

"Terribly."

So we called.

"Hello," said Grandma.

"Hello," we replied.

"Quickly," said Grandma away from the phone. "Come to me, children. It's Mommy and Daddy on the telephone."

Little voice in background: "I'm too busy."

Other little voice: "Bababababa."

Grandma: "Children! Don't you miss Mommy and Daddy?"

Little voice: "No."

Other little voice: "Bababababa."

Grandma (to us): "They send love and kisses – but they're too shy to come to the phone."

"Where did we go wrong?" my wife sobbed later.

"Never mind, we still have each other," I consoled.

I think she cried even harder.

99

From his regular platforms in Star Weekly *and* Weekend
*magazines, Greg Clark probably reached more
Canadians than any humorist since Leacock. His
artist friend Jimmy Frise always depicted him a little
fatter than fact. When readers gently inquired if all his
stories were true, the puckish Clark replied:*
"What a question to ask!"

100

Hi There!

BY GREG CLARK

It is with natural reluctance that I admit that I have been a toffee addict for sixty-some years.

But it is necessary to do so to explain all that excitement and confusion at my front door yesterday, that police cruiser, those two doctors, five minutes apart, dashing up the walk with their bags.

Racial prejudice inclines me toward Scotch toffee. But it is not as sticky as English treacle toffee. Treacle toffee has that same virtue that is referred to when they say a food sticks to the ribs. Treacle toffee sticks to the teeth. Many a time I have gone to sleep at night with a good gob of treacle toffee glued to my molars. And when I woke in the morning, there it was, still. I had been enjoying it in my dreams.

My vice was discovered early in my childhood, and my parents tried every device to wean me to other candies. Chocolates? I have no use for them. One squish with your tongue against the roof of the mouth and they're gone.

Though I am naturally of a vivacious and extroverted nature, I was thought, through my childhood, to be a rather speechless and taciturn boy. This was because my mouth was locked shut on a hunk of treacle toffee.

School teachers often clouted me over the head because I apparently was a rebellious pupil, stubbornly refusing to answer a question. I answered as soon as I could.

I am giving you these details so that you will appreciate what happened yesterday. Many of my neighbours have telephoned since then, and I have given them the true story. But I have no doubt that those who saw the excitement and did not telephone me will have spread the news all over that I have suffered a stroke, or broken my neck, or some such rumour.

Actually, the best toffee I ever encountered in a long epicurean life, as far as toffee goes, was Belgian. In one of those wars, I helped capture a small Belgian village. And in pollacking around the ruins, as soldiers do, I found this small tin box, in what likely had been the *patisserie* of the village. It contained the most delectable toffee I have ever consumed. You could

101

clamp a piece of that toffee in your teeth and inhale it for three-quarters of an hour. The label was burned off the box, of course. Some of my friends have since become ambassadors to Belgium, trade commissioners, and so forth. I have had them scour the whole of Belgium. They never came up with it.

Another mighty toffee I met about 15 years ago when I was down in Tennessee and Arkansas trying to buy a good beagle. Our car got stuck in the mud, and an old Negro mammy invited us into her shanty while she sent her grandson afoot in quest of a tow truck. She served us coffee and gave us a treat of her homemade toffee made with sorghum. I tell you, if I had been a man of means, I would have established that old mammy in Manchester, England, or Doncaster, or one of the great shrines of treacle toffee, and she would have made a fortune for us. I would probably be a peer of the realm, by now, like those mustard lords, biscuit lords and liver-pill lords they have over there.

But in every life some rain must fall. In my fifties, I had to surrender my teeth and adopt dentures. There are those, I know, who would say that no teeth could withstand the pull, drag and wrench of half a century of toffee chewing. But my dentist tells me this is nonsense. In my case, it was more likely chewing on pipe stems, gnawing venison rib chops and munching radishes.

The shock with which I discovered that my toffee days were over, apparently, was one of the dark moments of my life. I put the usual gob of toffee in. And I nearly smothered. You can't take BOTH dentures out at the same time. And my two were cemented together.

I just soaked it through. Thereafter, for three years, by shrewdly selecting quite small splinters of toffee, I developed a certain skill. And of course, by now, I can handle the usual-size chunk. But naturally, it enjoins a period of silence each time.

Last week, my womenfolk went on a motor trip down to the States, they having not been over the border for four months, and each of them having $25 burning holes in their purses. And I was left at home here alone with Chelsea, our Corgi dog.

My sister, who lives in the country, thought she would just give me a long-distance ring to see how I was making out.

"How are you making out?" she asked brightly, when I picked up the receiver.

"Fine," I said.

But, as I had a large gob of toffee just nicely snuggled in my molars, it came out:

"Bhmmmm!"

"What's that?" she exclaimed.

"I'll call you back later," I said.

But it came out:

"Bobgumbagbmmmmm!"

"Greg!" cried my sister.

"Aw, for Peter's sake," I said, "I'll ring you back in about 15 minutes."

But it came out:

"Gombungbeebungbaaaahhhh!"

At which moment, Chelsea found a late autumnal bee bumping around the floor, and she burst into frantic barks, for she has a high horror of bees.

"Ggmmmmm!" I yelled at her, to keep her quiet.

"Oh, you poor man!" cried my sister, and hung up.

I squashed the bee and walked around the house for a little while until the toffee had subsided enough. Then I put a call through to my sister's farm.

The line was busy.

I was debating whether to take another chunk of toffee, for there were only two pieces left on the plate, when the doorbell rang loudly, and somebody at the same time rapped violently on the same door.

I opened.

It was two policemen.

"You, Mr. Clark?"

"Yes, sir."

"All O.K. here?"

"Yes, sir."

"We had an emergency call," said the constable. "Said you were ill. Possibly a stroke."

"Me?" I protested.

So I invited them in and cracked up another cake of toffee and gave them a treat. We were just nicely settled into it when again the doorbell rang.

This was the first doctor. A stranger to me.

"I had an emergency call from the country," he said. "Mr. Clark?"

"Yes, sir."

"Are you all O.K.?"

"Yes, sir."

"They said you must have suffered a stroke."

So he joined the two policemen, and we were all sitting having some toffee when the second doctor, who is my own doctor, arrived. They had got him at the hospital, and he had rushed right up. (We fish together, and a doctor doesn't like to lose a fishing companion.)

About an hour later, if you were still watching, you saw my sister arrive.

By this time the doctors and the police had left.

"Have some toffee," I suggested to my sister, when she had recovered her breath and poise.

"No, THANK you!" she said.

THE OCCASIONAL HUMORISTS

COLUMNIST MCKENZIE PORTER AND FRIEND.

The best humour is often a paragraph, chapter, introduction to an essay, or a newspaper column by a writer who is not a humorist in particular but has a wonderful sense of humour and lets it go now and then. At any rate, here are some bits and pieces that, for one reason or another, I have enjoyed.

SCOTT YOUNG

I find myself blushing rosily even to mention this matter, but I must. Crooked sewing machine repairmen are not the only blights on our society that should be rooted out, stamped on, exterminated, by a fearless crusading columnist. It is in this context, one of duty alone, that I address myself to readers who carry handbags (most of whom, even in this enlightened city, are women) and issue this warning:

When in any large public place you go to a powder room whose partitions do not extend to the ceiling, do not hang your handbag on one of those hooks often found high on the inside of the door.

I know, I know – your first reaction must be deep reflection. Without knowing precisely what I am driving at, you are trying to work out the logistics of how you could possibly manage all that has to be done without hanging up your handbag. I can only promise that I will attempt to help you with these problems as soon as I have explained why I am bringing up the matter at all.

Now, I'm only telling you something I heard, and have been unable to authenticate. But it is plausible and goes as follows.

A woman shopper went into the powder room at a large department store. She hung her handbag on the hook. Being wise in the larcenous ways of public washrooms, she gathered all her parcels on the floor close around her feet and had her spike heels ready to stamp on any attempt to grab these parcels and haul them into a neighboring cubicle or the public area outside.

While thus alert and ready, suddenly a movement caught her eye. A hand appeared over the top of the door, darted swiftly to the hook and grabbed her handbag, which then soared out of sight.

I must draw a veil over her subsequent feverish activity and the attendant problems, but suffice it to say that when she was decently able to wrench open the door and plunge out crying for help, the thief had disappeared and so had her handbag, with all her money, keys, and 524 miscellaneous items.

She reported this event to the store detective. He promised that if the handbag were found, she would be informed.

The next day she received a telephone call. A woman identifying herself as Miss Hibbletwaite (or something) from the store said the bag had been found, all money gone, everything else intact, and when could she pick it up?

They made a date for 4 p.m. that day. She went down and was told there was no Miss Hibbletwaite and her handbag had not been found. Puzzled and frustrated, she went home – and found that her apartment had been ransacked. Apparently the thief or an accomplice had made the call, had known from papers in the handbag where she lived, had known she would be out at the certain time, and had used her own keys to get in and burgle her place.

As you can see, then, it really would be worth while to figure out a system for going to a powder room which would not involve hanging up your handbag.

But, anticipating that some women might sob helplessly that it can't be done, I have a few other ideas.

The most simple, I think, involves hockey sticks. Almost everyone buys at least one hockey stick at Christmas. My suggestion is that if you fall into this category, buy it first. Then, if you must hang up your handbag, as soon as you get settled take a good two-handed grip on the hockey stick and hold it over your shoulder as Mickey Mantle might so in a similar situation. The moment a hand appears – wham!

One other possibility that might both save the handbag and catch the thief would have special appeal to those ladies whose gifts run more to fishing tackle than hockey sticks. Get a 30-pound test line and tie it to the handbag before you hang it up. You might feel silly sitting there, rod ready, the reel set at full drag – but remember, no one will see you. And if you get a strike all you have to do is set your feet and reel.

Any other questions?

LADY CHATTERLEY, LATTERLEY

BY WALTER O'HEARN

Being determined upon a literary career, I began with biography and research and came up with a plum. The true story of Lady Chatterley.

I do not mean the book, which in 1961 ceased to be an illicit joy in England and several parts of the Commonwealth. (Not, however, in New Zealand; not, however, in Quebec; certainly not in Manitoba, where they talk about banning Hugh MacLennan.) The book is the indiscreet memoir D. H. Lawrence wrote about two indiscreet friends, and you may take it or leave it.

I'm talking about the girl herself.

To use a phrase embodied in amber by generations of diplomatic correspondents, I am in a position to reveal, for the first time in print, what happened to Constance Chatterley, latterly.

This information was gathered at great pains by a team of private inquiry agents. Their diligent researches in the United Kingdom, France, Italy, and Switzerland were hampered by the fact that Lawrence, in a rare access of discretion, had slightly altered the names of the lovers. Since this literary device has acquired the grip of legend, I shall use the names chosen by the novelist.

Sir Clifford Chatterley, Bart., was granted a decree *nisi* in the autumn of 1924. This decree was made absolute six months later, in spite of the best efforts of the King's Proctor. Constance Chatterley and Mellors, the ex-gamekeeper, were married under special licence in the following week. After a wedding luncheon held at the Kensington Palace Hotel, which was attended only by the bride's father and sister, the blissful couple took train and boat for the Continent, where they settled into lodgings at Menton.

Mellors, who had, as Lawrence took pains to remind us, held the King's commission, was on his best behaviour during this interlude. The Derbyshire dia-lect which had been so effective in his courtship was rightly judged unsuitable for the pension-dwellers of Menton, but Mellors, as readers of the novel will remember, could slip into standard English as easily as he could into neatly-brushed town clothes. This he did.

In other ways, Mellors did not fit. His experience in the regimental mess in India had bred in the game-keeper a stubborn refusal to accommodate himself to the ways of a class he despised. He loved the meal known as high tea and despised continental cookery. He was prone to thump the table with his knife to emphasize a point in conversation. Being addicted to monosyllables he took to addressing his wife as "Con," which she resented. Violent arguments in their bed-sitting-room after dinner disturbed the other boarders at Villa Mon Repos, and the Mellorses were asked to move.

They moved to Var, where Wilberforce Gresham Mellors was born. (These were not family names. The little fellow was named for Bishop Wilberforce and the author of Gresham's Law.) Because of Mellors' increasing intractability they were asked to move again. After a brief, unhappy stay in Paris, in a hotel on the Boulevard Raspail, they settled down in a villa outside Geneva.

It was Constance who chose the capital of Swiss virtue. Years later she said that she made the choice because the schools were good and young Wilberforce must have the best. Constance was a being who made an unabashed and total commitment to every new relationship and she was from the outset a possessive and dedicated mother. This brought an immediate and unsubtle change in her relationship with Mellors. Gone was the easy camaraderie, and the endearments that went therewith.

Mellors responded to the dilemma in the only way he knew. For a time there were whispers about him and a comely widow who worked in the League of Nations secretariat. Soon these ugly rumours reached Connie's ears and she dealt with them in her firm Scots way. After all, she reminded Mellors, she had given up a great deal for him. After all, she held the purse.

This was true. As her father, Sir Malcolm Reid, R.A., had reminded the gamekeeper, "She has her own income: moderate, but above starvation." Some years later Sir Malcolm died, leaving his paintings to an ungrateful nation and his remaining funds to his younger daughter.

Thus replenished, the Mellorses were able to survive the 1930s' slump and the lower yield of investments. Nevertheless, the living was lean. Mellors had

105

to abandon his cherished dream of entering Wilberforce in a public school, giving him opportunities which he had been denied. Years of idleness had eroded the rebellious streak in Mellors. He forgot his Derbyshire accent, took to dressing for dinner, and revived his military title, promoting himself to field rank.

Having scraped along until 1939 well above the squalor line, the Mellorse's were summoned home by the second war. Mellors, no shirker, tried to join up. He was rebuffed when he sought a commission. (Sir Clifford had died, but his War Office pals remembered.) In 1940, aged fifty-five, he managed to re-enlist as a private in the Army Service Corps. He worked his way through the ranks again and 1945 found him a captain, deputy R.T.O. at Folkstone. Wilberforce was drafted in 1944. Connie sat through the war in Battersea.

By now she had taken up Theosophy, was given to talking aloud to herself, and was thought by the neighbours to be peculiar. When Mellors was demobilized, he found this new taste unbecoming, but since he himself was addicted to something known as the prophecies of the pyramids, he was in no position to complain. Years of exposure in an embarkation shed had left him permanently crippled by arthritis and had not improved his disposition.

After a year with the Army of Occupation, Wilberforce Mellors entered a commercial college. (When last encountered he was prospering as an accountant in Vancouver.) His parents moved to a semi-detached house in Hove, thence to Bognor, thence to a private hotel in Bournemouth, thence and finally to a nursing home.

You will now and then see them on a fair day, the woman of sixty-five with a sweet, sagging face, wheeling the pale slim man with a sweeping moustache, who growls at her from his bath chair and occasionally, in a change of tone, mutters senile Saxon endearments.

Years on the Continent had veiled from the Mellorses the long controversy which raged about D. H. Lawrence's book. They weren't great readers in any case.

Last month an infirmary attendant bought a copy of the Penguin edition of the unexpurgated Lady Chatterley, which he lent to Captain Mellors.

"G-rr-ah. Frightful book," the Captain cried, hurling the volume at the wall.

Constance, firmly returning the book to its owner, was more tactful.

"I'm sure it's very interesting," she said. "But – don't you think – too stimulating. And not really nice."

BARRY MATHER

"Ghost-walkers," police dressed as civilians, are mingling with and watching pedestrians as they cross Vancouver streets. (NEWS ITEM)

DIRTY WORK AT THE CROSSWALKS

Dramatis Personae:
Pounce – a Ghost-walker
Old Lady – a Pedestrian
Swivel – the Same
SCENE 1: A street in Vancouverum
Pounce: Oft doth the tarnished cup contain a wine of virtue. Aye, and good they say that's done by evil is yet still good. But beneath these, the habilments of disguise, my heart leaps not. Nay, though I save a hundred by betraying ten, I like it not . . . But soft!
Enter: *Old Lady*: Come! Quick, ere 'walk' goes 'wait'! How fleeting is the time officialdom hath left for ancient legs to cheat a furious traffic! Fie! 'tis 'wait' again. Yet cross I will. Who'll stop me? Who, I say?
Pounce: Hold, dame! Backward to the curb, where safety lies. A word I'd have with thee. (*Grasps her arm.*)
Old Lady: Oh, shame! In these, our peaceful streets, is woman not yet safe? Unhand me, villain! The Watch I'll set upon thee!
Pounce: Peace good grandma. A disguised officer of the Watch I myself am, and . . .
Old Lady: A bull in wolf's clothing? Thou liest! I know thou liest. Wicked villain!
(*Exits, calling "Help! Police!"*)

Pounce: From mad dames protect us. Yet, let her go. Her 'walking' days are short, I trow. But who comes here?'

(*Enter Swivel*)

Swivel: The sun upon his golden path has reached the zenith of his arch. 'Tis time that men should slake the dust from their enparched throats. I'll cross to yonder tavern. (*Jay walks*)

Pounce: Halt! thou illegitimate crosser!

Swivel: Now, who art thou to so command?

Pounce: Hast thou not read how, to protect the citizenry from such as thee, a troop of police do, in deep disguise, keep secret vigil in the streets? One of these am I, a sergeant of the Ghost-walk Corps.

Swivel: (*thinking quickly*): Why, comrade, so am I. Thy disguised brother officer, newly joined, I do but jay-walk to gull those whose crimes I'll spot – and thus catch sinners at their sinning. Farewell, comrade! To our work! Farewell! (*Exits*)

Pounce: Hmmmmmmmmmm.

✤✤✤✤

McKenzie Porter

London's eight million denizens live like the cells in frog spawn, in a teeming, frigid, palpitating propinquity, in a vast togetherness of isolations that sometimes becomes so intolerable it erupts into the most ghoulish murders of our times. Kippered by smog, mildewed by rain and tousled by daily strap-hanging, Londoners return from their jobs to toast their chilblains around fierce little fires that heat but a corner of those glacial caves they call every man's castle. Icy bathrooms discourage most Londoners from more than one tub a week. Rube Goldbergish laundry rooms perpetuate an enormous sale of shirts with detachable collars, a device that permits the major garment to be worn two or three times without washing. A crease in the pants is so difficult to preserve in London's dank homes, that most people give up trying.

The dark, narrow terrace house of the average Londoner smells of cats, yesterday's cabbage and the old leather campaign trunk that great-granddad brought back from Omdurman. The stamp-sized backyard of the typical London dwelling, sprouting its incongruous culture of roses, radishes, carnations and cauliflowers, is enclosed by a high brick wall that intensifies the warren-like nature of metropolitan existence.

From tiny garages there emerges erratically onto London's streets such an ear-splitting, bone-shaking assemblage of scooters, bubble-buggies, motorcycle-sidecars, three-wheel runabouts and other midget rattletraps that the annual London-to-Brighton Veteran Car Run comes as an amazing demonstration of mechanical sanity.

Londoners still drink coffee adulterated with the dried roots of chicory, a fleshy, blue-flowered weed that thrives in highway ditches and is used otherwise to bulk out cheap cattle fodder. They still eat sausages so full of old bread and minced animal muscles that such sausages were prohibited from sale in the British Pavilion at the Brussels World Fair by the same Belgian health authorities who blithely sanction for orphanage dinner tables the meat of sway-backed horses. At the railroad stations Londoners still gnaw like rodents on buns that have hardened for days under flyblown glass covers. And in the average London café the waitresses still look as though they've slept all night on the kitchen floor.

Oh yes, life in London can set on edge the teeth of Canadians, even New Canadians like myself. I cleared out of London years ago and came to Canada where I bask blissfully in centrally heated cleanliness, in functional plumbing, in man-sized automobiles and in the appetizing vision of herds of fat steak beasts meandering endlessly up the ramps to the abattoirs.

Yet every now and then, darn it, I find myself called back to London by an irresistible voice . . . I am called back by Fleet Street where I committed the folly of becoming a journalist; by the West End, in whose theatres, cabarets and restaurants I tried to forget that doltish act; and by Richmond, the ancient suburb where I took in wedlock Kathleen and begat Timothy, the wife and son who for more than twenty years have shared the absurdities of my inkslinging life . . .

Once . . . I went up to a smart part of Chelsea where an old friend of mine, now a titled woman, lives with her husband. She spends a lot of her time carrying buckets of coal up the flights of carpeted stairs and carrying buckets of ashes down, and she shivers whenever she leaves the semicircle of chairs and chesterfields huddled around the main fireplace.

"Why don't you live in a place like Litchfield Court, Richmond?" I asked. "It's just like living in Canada."

"For Heaven's sake!" she snapped. "Don't be so bloody bourgeois!"

She had me there. I'm bourgeois, as well as a Philistine. And with this thought, I returned to Canada . . .

Professor John Satterly mixed laughter and learning. He would dance and sing or mime – anything to trap a student's wavering attention to his science lectures.

Laughs in liquid air

One of the most entertaining shows ever put on in Canada was a lecture on liquid air given annually in the 1940s to first-year science students at the University of Toronto by Professor John Satterly, one of the top teachers of physics in North America.

Professor Satterly appeared in the lecture room wearing the cap and gown of a doctor of science, University of London, and with a dead-pan expression and with the gestures of a stripper began to remove it, acknowledging the students' hilarious shouts of "more" with a couple of passes at his vest. He produced an Anglican hymn book, sang "Thou moon that rul'st the night, and sun that guid'st the day. Ye glittering stars of night. To Him you homage pay. His praise declare. Ye heavens above. And clouds that float on liquid air," and emptied a vessel of liquid air into a jar, making a tremendous vapour cloud, so that he appeared to be floating on liquid air himself. He went offstage, reappeared in an air-raid warden's helmet, carrying a torch and began to make and detonate bombs made of liquid oxygen and waste, setting tin cans over the charge and touching them off. At one point he ignited a ring of asbestos gauze, put it on his head, turned out the lights and marched around the room in the attitude of prayer, his face illuminated by a brightly burning halo.

Satterly had a repertoire of jokes, many of them about engineers, which he sharply distinguished from scientists. "You can't equate apples to oranges, inches to seconds, or engineers to physicists," and he put the problems that he set for his class in his own colorful imagery. "The dead body of an engineer was being dragged across the campus." "A certain professor lay in his bath watching a towel slip off a rack." "A certain baby was thrown out a window onto a fine English lawn."

Some of Professor Satterly's colleagues objected to his horseplay, but most of the faculty followed his antics with fond amusement and admiration, and physics classes have never since enjoyed such enthusiastic attendance.

GEORGE BAIN

BOSTON (AP) *A psychological study of married women has found that women who enjoy food the most are also better able to enjoy sex.*

"I think," he said, "some oysters first,
Or is it cherrystones for you?
And something cool to slake our thirst
– The Chablis Vaudesir should do;
I think, perhaps, you'd like the steak
With artichoke (au gratined heart),
And after that, some sort of cake
Or (do I dare suggest it?) tart;"
She smiled: "You know, I can't recall
That any time I've dined with men,
I've had a taste for food at all."
– He never took her out again.

John Clare

I know some Canadian husbands who feel that the scientists who are working to create a cleaner H-bomb (so that if the world does go mad enough, the end will come not with a whimper but with a nice clean bang) could make an even greater contribution to mankind. They could sit down for a minute and work out a simple answer to the question – "Why didn't you phone?"

Some husbands, of course, arrive home from work at the same time every night. They never forget to pick up small forgotten items at the corner store and they hit the front porch purged of all the cares of the day, brimming with anecdotes, many of them true, with which to answer their wives who have been stuck in the house all day. The scientists don't need to worry about those husbands too much, because I just made them up.

The husbands who need the scientists' help are men like Henry Blodgett. Henry's of medium height, a little pudgy, quite pleased with himself, worried about his weight but not enough to stop stuffing himself, fond of fishing, fond of talk, kind to animals, selfish and so on. He could be described as an average Canadian husband but just try describing him that way to his face and he will probably swing at you – and probably miss. It was his love of talk, mainly his own, that got Henry into the situation that forms the burden of our essay. He was ready to leave his office, shortly before five, when he got this call from George Framish. Framish, who was now located in Winnipeg, he said, wanted Henry to come down to the hotel for a drink.

"Sure," Henry replied without hestitation and then sat back and made a face at himself. He and Framish had known each other overseas and had never had much use for each other. Year after year, Henry had gone along without ever thinking of him except once when he thought he saw Framish's picture in a newsreel shot of a police raid.

Now, just like that, it had become important that he go all the way down to the hotel which was not on the way home unless he planned to go by way of Cleveland. Why? Perhaps because it was five o'clock, an uncomplicated but puissant reason. Perhaps it was because Framish had talked with the hearty glibness of a man on a big expense account. On the way out

the door Henry asked himself if he should have phoned home. "Sure," he replied in that incisive way of his. But it really didn't make any difference because he was just going for a minute.

When he got to the hotel room Henry had to sit on the luggage rack because all the good chairs and beds had been taken by Framish's other guests. He was given a drink and a puzzled look by his host who had obviously thought he had phoned someone else. After all, twelve years is a long time and even old enemies can drift apart.

The room was full of smoke and talk and George was demanding and getting his full privilege as a host. Like a kid I knew who owned the baseball and always insisted on pitching. Henry was miserably uncomfortable. The luggage rack bit into him cruelly and the sound of George's voice was making his head swim. Besides it was time he was starting home. It wasn't fair to keep dinner waiting, not to mention his wife. But as he got up, George went to the door and a kind of hush fell over the room. What better time to tell his story about the town major and the Italian countess, Henry decided.

Even Framish seemed amused by the story, which he would undoubtedly record and reissue in Winnipeg as his own. Henry regarded him with distaste. He must have been out of his mind to come all the way downtown to see him. But here he was throwing his arm around Henry's shoulder and talking about getting some Chinese food. And when Henry glanced instinctively at his watch, Framish loudly demanded to know if he was afraid of his wife.

Henry threw back his shoulders, took a deep breath and gave the padding of his jacket a chance to settle. What, he asked, did Framish think he was?

Well, that was the situation. There is no need to look in on the sordid scene that developed when Framish engaged the waiter in a bitter argument over his interpretation of the dinner for four for three and the special dinner for two for one. And there's no need to recall the long and interesting discussion Henry had with his wife later that night when she asked, "Why didn't you phone?"

Henry didn't know why he hadn't and it's possible that not even a psychiatrist could tell her. So the scientists when they start to work will have to deal with a problem heavily weighted with thoughtlessness, a touch of rebellion, a spot of pride and many other flaws that are found in the average decent adult male delinquent like Henry.

Good luck, men, and when you get X to equal something reasonably plausible you can reach Henry care of us. He's waiting to hear from you.

A
SONG
IN
SUPERLATIVES

BY NATHANIEL A BENSON

And now, men, Joe Mustard will tell you all about IT,
Our 1938 Product!
You've all heard Joe before –
He needs no introduction –
Joe!!
This, at last, when I lifted up my longing eyes,
Was the true Apotheosis of Big Business,
Commerce come into Her Own –
Of such is the 1938 Kingdom of Heaven!
Crouching, straightening up,
Bending, leaning, imploring,
Prancing, pounding, punching home,
Rivetting home FACTS!
Big Facts! – Whole Facts!! – Money Facts!!
Science become belligerent, bombastic Business,
Big business – and when I say 'Big,'
I don't mean just 'BIG,' –
I mean 'BETTER THAN EVER BEFORE!!
WOW!!! COLOSSAL!!!!'

Solemn, big-faced, best-tailored, bevel-chinned,
Sedan-owning men faced Joe,
Agape, agog, aglow,
Envying that Hitlerian flow
of unquenchable ardour and eloquence.
He roared – he stamped – he swore manfully –
Denton, Burke, Bossuet, Billy Sunday,
Yes, even the pebble-sucking Demosthenes
Gargled through his honest healthy howls.
He worshipped, drunk with the fierce ardour
Of a Baalite, a Sun-Worshipper,
An Eleusinian Bacchanal,
A Maenad shrilling "Evoe!"
But the big, smooth, spotless, stainless

Cabinet of Cold
Stood,
Bannered like the Assyrian in purple and gold,
'Better Than Ever Before!'
Stood austere, remote and quiet,
Chill and correct as a Japanese apology.
Streamlined in Chromium,
Perfect in mechanism,
The ultimate, last word in Refrigeration,
Complete with Hydrator, Meter Miser, Kuberkliker,
Divine in the Still, Silent Snootiness of its own
        goddamned Mechanical Snobbishness,
With a Silver Medallion Superimposed
'Father's Gift to the Family, 1938,'
Half-suggesting that
Father was Inside
On the quiet Top Shelf
Among the ninety-six self-removable cubes
Being Meter-misered, Hydrated, or Chilled,
Fast-frozen for that smooth-flowing, Final Fugue
Called the Last Trump . . .

There It stood,
Swathed like Sally Rand
In seven shining square yards of Cellophane,
Girdled with a gigantic Bow
Of Crimson Cellophane –
And as I listened to Joe
Wheedling, howling and cajoling
And looked at the Frigid Deity
In all of its impressive Impassivity
And voiceless Magnificence –
I arose, shouting my conversion. . . .
And bought the bloody thing myself!

THREE CHEERS FOR ME

BY DONALD LAMONT JACK

It was October before I got to France. After those miserable weeks on Salisbury Plain I was quite looking forward to the trenches and a little excitement. At last I was on my way to join the Victorian Light Infantry Regiment of the Tenth Canadian Division in reserve in the Albert Region. I was travelling with an acquaintance called Rupert Randle. Out of a group of 15 or so officers, we were the only ones who went up by train. The remainder somehow managed to arrange transport by motor car.

I had thought the troop train from Montreal to Halifax was crowded, but it did not compare with the train from Havre. It took us 15 minutes to negotiate only ten feet of corridor, wrenching our way through a solid wall of soldiers, some of whom were three deep on the floor. It was all very sordid.

We peered in one compartment after another, but they were jammed.

"Give it up, mon," a Scottish lieutenant whose leg we had trodden on advised us. "There's not a single seat left in the whole bliddy train."

But I went on searching. I had had to stand at the ship's rail during the entire crossing of the Channel on a small, filthy steamer, and I had heard that French trains were like snails. I was determined to get a seat.

My pertinacity was rewarded. I saw a space in the middle of a seat in the end compartment. It was an upholstered seat, too. I was just about to open the door when Rupert clutched my arm.

"It's reserved for senior officers," he shouted above the clatter of the wheels, as the train rushed headlong into the night at five miles an hour.

It was then I saw that the compartment was crammed with red tabs and brassards. At least two of the occupants were generals. My heart sank as I pressed my nose against the glass and peered longingly in at the luxurious, smoke-filled interior. But I could see no sticker on the window indicating that the compartment was reserved.

They were all talking and laughing. They seemed to be having a good time. I gazed wistfully at the space in the middle of one of the seats. The officers on each side were taking up a lot of room, but the space was still many inches wide, and it was upholstered. After all, I thought, why not?

"Why don't you take that seat, Rupert?" I said. "The compartment isn't officially reserved."

Rupert shuddered slightly. "Not me," he said.

"Then I'm going to."

He seized my arm. "You're not!"

"Why not? They're not ogres. Look, see? They're laughing."

"In with *them*?"

"Why not?"

"You can't! They're generals!"

"I don't see why I should stand when there's a seat."

"Don't be a fool, Bandy!"

I clutched the door for support. The door slid open and I half fell into the compartment.

Five pairs of eyes stared at me. I turned to go out again, but someone had already closed the door. I was trapped. After a momentary panic I decided there was nothing else for it but to stay. It would have been impossible to get back to the corridor anyway, the doorway was so jammed with bodies. I turned and nodded politely; then on an afterthought I tried to salute but succeeded only in rapping my knuckles painfully on a wooden panel.

They had all stopped talking, all staring hard. There was a pair of legs stretched across the compartment belonging to a major. He made no effort to move them. I stepped over them carefully. I flung my valise onto the baggage rack and threw my trench coat on top of it. It fell off. I just managed to catch it, stumbling a little over another outstretched pair of legs.

"Sorry," I said.

The dead silence continued. There was not even the sound of breathing.

With infinite care I lowered myself into the upholstered space between the two gentlemen on the right.

Opposite I saw a lieutenant colonel and two brigadiers. I glanced quickly toward my right. In the window position I met a gaze so frigid that I shuddered visibly. It belonged to a full lieutenant general. On my right was a staff major. He had an ice-cold aristocratic face and two buck teeth.

Every one of them continued to stare at me.

"Good evening," I said. The brigadiers seated opposite started.

I must admit I was acutely uncomfortable. The general and the major on each side of me were generously spread out on the seat, leaving me practically no room. I realized that my buttocks were barely touching the seat.

These officers were making not the slightest effort

to move over, although they had plenty of room. The major in particular was leaning at an angle so that there was a good six inches between him and the end of the seat. I felt a little annoyed about that. I started to wiggle, and gradually felt myself sinking between them until finally I was in contact with the upholstery.

It was a tight fit but a great improvement.

The silence continued for another minute. There was still not even the sound of breathing. They hadn't taken their eyes off me since my abrupt arrival.

"That's better," I said conversationally.

The brigadier opposite started again.

"Facing the engine, I mean," I went on. "I always like to face the engine."

The brigadier opposite gave this some thought, for the glassy look left his eye. He blinked. It was the first movement I had seen. I was very grateful for that blink.

But the deathly silence continued. I cleared my throat.

One of them started to hum, and I was pleased to note that it was a hymn tune. I recognized it immediately. It was *Rock of Ages*. I looked around approvingly to see who was humming it when I met the gaze of the general. The tune died away immediately, and it was only then that I realized it was I who had been humming.

The merciless silence continued. They had all been talking loudly before I came in. Perhaps, I thought, they had been discussing military secrets.

After three more bloodcurdling minutes, during which the others not only did not speak but did not even blink again, I reached up for my valise, took it

down, opened it, and took out my large, heavy Bible, replaced the valise, and discreetly crushed myself back between the major and the general. I tried very hard to avoid digging them in the ribs as I opened the Good Book. Wetting my left thumb and forefinger, I turned over the pages until I came to an interesting part, and began to read.

Turning the second page, I happened to glance up, and could not repress a start, because whereas before the surrounding faces had seemed to express an outraged reserve, they now mirrored a stupefied astonishment. They kept looking from me to the, I must admit, rather large volume, then from the volume back to me, as if they had never seen a Bible before. To make matters worse, I now needed to go to the lavatory.

For the first time I began to doubt whether I had been wise to leave home. I reminded myself that they were, after all, high officers and had many cares and worries on their minds. The whole conduct of the war, I told myself firmly, depended on these intellects. So I forgave the unpleasant silence.

By now I needed quite badly to relieve myself. But I was determined not to leave, knowing full well that I'd never get back in again.

Still, it would have been nice to have heard a little of their conversation. For persons of such exalted rank it could hardly fail to be full of scintillating talk, full of worldly and military subtlety.

And finally they did speak. It was round about Etaples, I think.

"I hear old Farthing-Prebble's got XXX, sir," the brigadier in the window seat mumbled to the general next to me.

"Old Farthing-Prebble of G.2 (D)?"

"Yerser, G.2 (D)D2, sir."

"G.2(D)D2, XD.A.Q.M.G., dig-dig got XXX?"

"MY word, top hole! XXX, A?" someone else added.

"Taff Div. H.Q. Promul. G.2 (D) last wik, ih? Yes."

"By gad! What about Grunty C.B.R.E. X D. A.D.O.S. um?"

"Gone sir, GSO.3 ups G.H.Q. Reserve CCN, bai gad."

"My word . . . 'member old G. with his penchant for 0.3 Umblryon, eh, eh? Ha!"

"Ha!"

The general and the brigadier general laughed briefly. I was looking from one to the other with a pleasant smile, trying to make out what they meant. The general had his mouth open and was about to add something when he saw me grinning. His mouth closed and he glared. Everyone subsided, and the silence settled in again more thickly than ever.

I don't know what it was that prompted me to contribute a few words myself. Perhaps it was through a belief that even generals might like to discuss ordinary, common or garden subjects as a relief from the intellectual altitude of high strategy. Or maybe it was because I was trying to take my mind off my own physical distress.

Anyway, I said, "What's it like at the front, sir?" to the B.G. in the corner. I chose him because he seemed to own the least unfriendly face.

They all looked at me again, startled. The B.G. seemed to have difficulty taking in the fact that I had actually addressed him.

After a moment he said, "What?"

"The front, sir. You see, I've never been there. I'm straight out from Canada."

"Canada?" he said, blinking.

"Yes, sir. You know. Dominion of Canada. Across the Atlantic."

"Atlantic?" the B.G. said blankly.

"Atlantic Ocean, sir. Took us two weeks to get across. Came over on the S.S. *Dismalia*."

"*Dismalia*?" the Brigadier said incredulously.

"A large passenger boat it was. We all slept in hammocks."

"Hamm –" the B.G. began. Then he shook himself, blinked several times, and looked at the brigadier beside him. "What's the feller talkin' about, Cecil?" he asked.

There was a pause while the B.G. thought for a moment. Then he said gruffly, "Hammocks."

The other brigadier stared at him for a longish spell. "Oh," he said.

There was a sudden convulsive movement beside me. It was the general, turning his head.

"Hammocks?" he said loudly. "Who's talking about hammocks? What's that to do with old Farthing-Prebble?"

They all looked at me. The major on my left suddenly barked, "Well? Speak up, man!"

I stared at him, then at the others. I thought perhaps they had not properly adjusted themselves from some lofty military contemplation on tactical analysis. "I wasn't actually referring to Farthing-Prebble," I said. "In fact I don't even know where it is."

"Where what is?"

"Farthing-Prebble, sir."

"I want to get to the bottom of this," the lieutenant general said angrily. "Where do hammocks come in?"

"They don't actually come in, sir," the major said respectfully, "they're already there, in a manner of

speaking. They usually hang from the ceiling."

The general's eyes bulged. "Farthing-Prebble . . . hanging from the ceiling?" he shouted. "What's he doing there?"

"No, sir," the major said very respectfully, "one sleeps in them."

"I'll get to the bottom of this if it's the last thing I do!" the general shouted, thumping his knee with his fist. His face was becoming purple. I began to feel alarmed. "What I want to know is what the devil Farthing-Prebble is doing in a hammock! He's supposed to be taking over Thirty Corps!"

"If that's the kind of man he is," the brigadier in the corner said, "he ought to be sent back to Div."

"He certainly will be!" the general thundered. "Never heard anything like it in me life! Links!"

The colonel in the corner who had been asleep started violently and straightened up. "Yessir," he said, stretching his mouth and dilating his eyes to get them open properly.

"Take a note, Links!" the general shouted. "Farthing-Prebble! Thirty Corps! Out!"

"Right, sir," the colonel said, scribbling furiously in a tiny note-book.

"I'll not have any officers sleeping on the job," the general went on. "Hammocks, indeed! Keenness, alertness, discipline!" He subsided and muttered for a bit. He saw me staring at him, wide-eyed. He leaned forward and patted me on the knee.

"Good work," he said, nodding. "I'll remember that."

He lay back and closed his eyes. Then he opened them and looked fiercely around until he found me again.

"What's your name?"

"Bandy, sir. B.W., sir."

"Good work, Bandy," he said, and appeared to go to sleep instantaneously.

I looked at the colonel. I looked at the brigadiers. I looked at the major. They were all nodding approvingly at me.

After all, I thought to myself, it's just that I haven't been in the army long enough to grasp the nuances of these things. Probably I had misunderstood the entire conversation.

Yes, that must be it, I thought, and settled back with a sigh of contentment. Obviously the whole thing was something entirely beyond the comprehension of a lowly subaltern. I was half asleep before I realized that I had hardly any need to go to the bathroom any more. I sighed again, pleasurably, and drifted into slumber, surrounded by a major, a lieutenant colonel and three generals – my friends.

113

NOW YOU CAN ENJOY *indoors,* the delights of charcoal-broiled meats, chicken, game and spare-ribs with this amazing cast-iron indoor barbecue. Built to last for years, the new device allows you to hold "rainy-day" barbecue parties in the comfort of your home – yes, and even in winter! Don't let storms or unseasonable weather spoil your fun; invest in an indoor barbecue now! *Perfectly safe*: Cast-iron sheath prevents sparks, hot coals, etc., from harming your floor. *Absolutely smoke-free*: Ingenious arrangement of pipes conducts smoke through hole in roof, dissipating it harmlessly in outer air. Patented draft system allows maximum efficiency. Your friends will turn green with envy when you invite them to your Indoor Barbecue Party!

AMAZING NEW INSTRUMENT actually *does away* with clumsy dial system. No more sore fingers, no more broken nails, thanks to the "Speaker-phone!" Simply lift receiver and *speak* your number into the Magic Mouthpiece. In a few moments your party will answer. It sounds incredible, but modern science has actually perfected the system so that most homes will soon be equipped with the dial-less instrument. Radical new "upright" design places mouthpiece at actual mouth level. No stooping, squatting, bending or neck craning needed. Be the first in your neighborhood to own one!

HERE'S AN AMAZING NEW INVENTION that will help you improve your writing skills. Now you can write with a firm, clear line that never skips, yet changes in width as you shape the letters. The line is stronger, clearer than that produced by old-fashioned ball-point, thanks to a new patented stylus called a "nib." And here's an additional feature: you no longer need to replace cartridges. An ingenious sac within the pen contains a supply of writing fluid or "ink" which is sucked up by a simple filling action.

BOTHERED BY PERSISTENT HYDRO FAILURES? Then here's the modern invention you've been dreaming of! A completely wire-less rug cleaner that does not depend on electrical contact for efficiency. The product of years of research, it is simplicity itself to use! Simply move it briskly across your carpets, and *presto!* – the rotating miracle brushes do the rest! Move it to any room in the house without plugging it in: the rug cleaner will astonish you by continuing to operate without wire or cord. They said it couldn't be done – but here's proof that it can! Works even in houses that contain no electrical wiring.

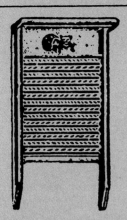

INGENIOUS NEW WASHING DEVICE is simplicity itself to operate . . . and fun, too! Guaranteed to contain no moving parts of any kind, it's the answer to the prayers of any housewife baffled by the intricacies of old-style washers. Nothing whatsoever can go wrong with the new do-it-yourself washer! Ingenious glass "riffles" scrub clothes whiter than white before your eyes, as you pass them across face of washer. And it's healthy exercise, recommended by leading doctors for over-weights and shut-ins. Well constructed and completely portable, it can be stored easily in kitchen cupboard when not in use.

HERE'S GOOD NEWS FOR HOUSEWIVES. Our new, ingenious freezer-refrigerator does away with defrosting-day blues, thanks to our new Custom Ice Delivery system which takes the drudgery out of freezer care. Think of it! No more filling pans with water! No more messy defrosting. Now *we bring the ice to you*! Yes, we actually deliver it to your door and place it in your refrigerator for as little as a few cents a week – scarcely more than you'd pay in electrical charges, with your old-fashioned 'frig. And here's an added feature: Custom 'Frig is completely sheathed in beautiful golden oak, especially designed to blend with modern panelled kitchens. Get rid of that "appliance look." Order a Custom Golden Oak Freezer-Frig today!

The man in the bunk above me

BY PIERRE BERTON

BERTON BY MACPHERSON

It is on May days like this one that I often wonder idly whatever became of a man whose name, I think, was Codweed. It was he who occupied the bunk directly above me during my first 10 weeks in the army. Then, on a May afternoon 18 years ago, our basic training period ended, and we were all scattered to the winds. I have not seen him since.

The army, of course, was like that. You could share a double-tiered bunk with a man for a period of months; eat with him, sleep with him and roust with him. Then, abruptly, it would be over.

In the course of my army life I grew to know some men better than I have known any man before or since. We shared secrets, bottles, money and girls. Yet they are only blurred memories today. Occasionally, I meet one on the street and we grope for names and places and dates, usually getting them wrong.

"Whatever happened to Dick Chambers? He get married or killed or what?"

"Dick Chambers? Was he the dark little one?"

"No – no! Fair and stocky. Tank corps. At Gordon Head he had the bed next to me, remember?"

"I was never at Gordon Head. We met at Petawawa, remember?"

"No. I was never at Petawawa."

115

"Oh. Then it must have been Brockville."

The memory of Codweed, however, is not blurred. I can see him today; thin-faced, sharp-nosed, gaunt and hollow-chested, slowly folding his blankets on the bunk above me. It is odd that he should stand out from all the others because I did not know him well. In fact, I did not know him at all.

The thing that first intrigued me about him was that he wrote a letter to his girl friend every single evening, and every single morning he got a letter in return. By letter I do not mean a cursory note or a couple of scribbled pages: I mean a tome, a White Paper, an immense brochure containing dozens of sheets inscribed in his tiny, cramped hand. It astonished me that any man would have so much to say. He should have been a columnist.

I think I understand him better now. Those letters were Codweed's only real life in the army. Everything else – the everlasting drill, the fatigue duty, the sham hate of bayonet practice – these things were a sort of mock life for Codweed. He lived vicariously in his letters. The rest of the time he was a sort of zombie, going through the motions.

I should explain that when it began we were all zombies. The army joined us: we did not join it. In that camp and at that time it was fashionable to be a zombie for the days of the great zombie persecution were yet to come. I can still recall how, at the end of the first week, three of us decided that we might just as well join Active Service and so we signed up and put up "Canada" badges and then ran the gantlet of 75 men in the hut all yelling "Sucker!"

No one else joined Active Service in that group. Like Codweed, they had no interest in war and none of the Larger Loyalties which the officers used to talk about. A decade of Canadian isolationism, anti-militarism and black depression had done its work. There were no patriots in that hut. The real loyalties were to home towns, families and girl friends to whom you wrote long letters every single day of the week.

Codweed had something seriously wrong with his back. I remember that he used to lie on his bunk and groan in the evenings. Indeed, after a few days he could not stand upright for much of the time and walked bent over, almost double.

He reported sick not once, but a dozen times or so, and in the army that took some doing. A man could be shaking with ague or burning with fever, but he still had to get fully dressed, put on his greatcoat, shoulder his pack and march off in step to the Medical Inspection Room. Here, the air was always blue with invalids coughing and cursing and spitting, and the chances were that if you weren't sick when you arrived you were sick when you departed. I reported sick just once and that was enough: but Codweed kept it up day after day.

The corporal and the sergeant and the Medical Officer and all the rest of the military hierarchy were terribly callous with Codweed. They refused to fix his back and kept sending him out on to the parade square where he could usually be seen limping a couple of paces behind the platoon.

He got a great deal of sympathy from the rest of us. In the evenings we would sit around his bed, shaking our heads, as he described his symptoms – the terrible pains that racked him, the nausea he felt when he was forced to march. We would all clench our fists and grit our teeth and curse the army which cared not a whit for human suffering. Codweed was our martyr and we took turns helping him on to the parade square.

Yet, as the days went on, we began to get a little weary of hearing the sergeant continually urging Codweed to keep in step. At first we hated the sergeant for persecuting Codweed, but after a while it became apparent that Codweed was holding the whole platoon back. He missed training because he was always on Sick Parade and as a result we missed break periods because the instructors were always helping Codweed to catch up.

Also there was a Platoon Competition being held in close-order drill and suddenly every man in our group desperately wanted to win it. Codweed had become a liability. The little knot of sympathizers around his bunk vanished. When he mentioned his back he got angry looks. On parade, when he missed step, the man behind would kick him. From martyr he graduated to pariah.

Then one day Codweed's back suddenly improved. He did not report sick. He went on parade and he even managed to stay in step. It was a miracle rivalling that of Lourdes.

There was no holding our platoon after that. Perfection in close-order drill became an obsession. It is hard to believe, after all these years, but we even practised it at night on our own time. And so we won the competition and were awarded a gold cup and had our photo taken and celebrated and swore eternal loyalty to one another.

The next day we broke up forever. It was an emotional leave-taking: I remember that several of our number cried openly. As I say, I have not seen or heard of Codweed since, but I do recall that when he became one of us during those final days he did not write his girl quite so often. I wonder if he married her?

REFLECTED GLORY

MacPherson

IN FRENCH OR ENGLISH

PRIMER FOR PARANOICS

See, see my motor car.
It is more than I can afford.
It can maim and kill, But I am
insured.

Look, look at the hydrogen bomb.
It can kill a lot of people. But it hasn't.
The motor car can kill a lot of people. It has.

"SHALL WE DANCE?"

Look, look at the lovely killways –
They cost 13 million dollars a mile.
Commuter railways are cheaper. Nobody
Likes them because they are safer.

See, see the impaired Angel.

NORRIS

Resolved, by the West Van Beautification and Adoration Society . . . that if the PGE is inevitable, it be made to conform to the local surroundings . . .

"No point in being beastly about Britain joining the Common Market . . . we'll jolly well become a bit of old France, old Germany, old Italy . . ."

THE VANCOUVER SUN

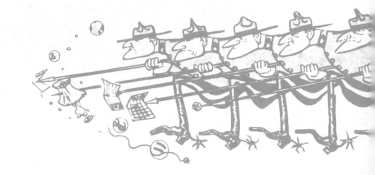

"What!! Modernise the Navy and abandon to blazes five hundred years of tradition!"

Whalley
CANADIAN HISTORY REVISITED

Laura Secord passes through the American lines.

Madeleine de Verchères defends her father's fort.

Champlain on Georgian Bay – 1615.

"If he calls me Jack once more . . ."

"Who's been eating my porridge?"

"Take them off! Do you want to end up in a
Russian circus?"

"Look, mister, I don't mind you watching, but take
your hot breath off the back of my neck!"

Feyer

Conclusion

Canadian humour has changed enormously in subject matter in the past quarter century. The hobo and the bootlegger have disappeared. The drunk still appears, but no longer just because he's drunk; he usually is an amusing contemporary psychological case. Kids no longer play hooky, go fishing and, rarely, thank heaven, sit behind hand-lettered signs with "Lemonade" misspelled. Women motorists don't have flat tires any more, and wouldn't dream of waiting for passing men motorists to stop and rescue them if they did. Young men no longer propose, on their knees or otherwise, or wait on the sofa for Mom and Pop to go to bed, or give the kid brother a nickel (a *nickel!*) to go away and buy something. The Queen and the Royal Family are now standard subjects of satire.

We've come a long way, agreed, but I think we face a danger. Until I began this book, I hadn't seen a college magazine or student paper for years. A young editor warned me: "You'll find student humour now is nearly all sacrilege and sex." He was right. He showed me an example from a current issue. There were no cartoons and there was hardly any written humour. There were photographs of pneumatic professional models and seasoned strippers. There was one photograph of a boy and a girl entwined on a lawn. The photographer had described his shot, explaining what they were doing and whose limbs you were looking at and from what angle, like a geologist describing the rock formations at Niagara Falls. The editor didn't laugh. It really wasn't funny. He didn't leer, either. He was completely factual and realistic about it and said that was what student papers went in for now. It was blood curdling.

I next phoned another university for some samples of *their* humour. I talked to the girl editor. It was refreshing to hear her young, polite and enthusiastic voice as she said *yes sir* she'd be glad to send me a copy of their special gag issue. A day later I sat bug-eyed reading what this sweet-voiced child had sent me. I stared at four-letter words and grotesque cartoons of women with Himalayan bosoms. It staggered me.

I was staggered even more when I attended a junior high school band concert in north Toronto a few days later. It was a remarkably good concert. When the music ended, someone announced that he wanted to present the conductor with a token of appreciation and, in front of 80 fresh-faced children, he wheeled out an arrangement of a life-sized model of a woman who appeared to be standing on her head in a tub giving birth to a bowl of fruit. I looked around half expecting to see the stage mobbed by enraged parents, but they sat there chuckling as if they'd just seen a bit of heart-warming nonsense from *The Wizard of Oz*.

What I've seen, I am convinced, is the beginning of an alarming reverse trend toward Victorianism, which mistook coarseness for humour. I hope the trend stops—fast. Coarseness is not new. It's not especially Canadian. It's certainly not humour.

Humour is difficult to define, but one thing is certain—it has nothing to do with denial of sensitivity, or the fact that a publisher is not afraid to say anything in print. It can be ribald, disrespectful, manic depressive, wry, cynical or sad, but it can never be ugly, plodding or in bad taste. It's a subtle, valuable, transient state of grace on loan to the human race, without guarantees of indestructibility, and now that Canadians have found it or, rather, demonstrated eminently that they always had it, they should make sure they don't lose it.

ACKNOWLEDGEMENTS

The excerpts in this book are reprinted with the kind permission of the following: From *Laughing with Lautens* by Gary Lautens; *Hi There* by Gregory Clark; *The Complete Poems of Robert Service* by permission of The Ryerson Press, Toronto; *The Ballad of Blasphemous Bill* by Robert Service from *The Collected Poems of Robert Service* by permission of The Ryerson Press, Ernest Benn Limited and Dodd, Mead & Company Inc.; *Sarah Binks* by P. G. Hiebert, by permission of Oxford University Press, © 1947; *One Man's Pilgrimage* by Nathaniel A. Benson by permission of Thomas Nelson & Sons (Canada) Limited and Mrs. Nathaniel Benson, © 1962; *In Pastures Green* and *The Red Cow and Her Friends* by Peter McArthur by permission of J. M. Dent & Sons (Canada) Limited; *Three Cheers For Me* by Donald Lamont Jack by permission of Collier-Macmillan Canada, Ltd. and The Macmillan Company, New York; *The Many Lives of Maggie Grant* by Maggie Grant, reprinted by permission of and published by Clarke, Irwin & Company, © 1964; *Lady Chatterley, Latterly,* by Walter O'Hearn by permission of the author and McClelland and Stewart Limited, © Walter O'Hearn, 1963; *Turvey* by Earle Birney, by permission of author and McClelland and Stewart Limited, © 1949; *The Clockmaker* by Thomas Chandler Haliburton and *The Stepsure Letters* by Thomas McCulloch by permission of Mc-Clelland and Stewart Limited; the *Globe and Mail* and *Needham's Inferno* by Richard Needham, by permission of the author and Macmillan Company of Canada, © Richard J. Needham 1966; *Jake and the Kid* by permission of the author W. O. Mitchell; from material from *Spring Thaw: Togetherness* by permission of the author Mavor Moore; *Dick and Jane*, 1962 by permission of the authors Gerry Ross and Marlene Perry; from *A Play on Words and Other Radio Plays* by permission of the author Lister Sinclair; the Toronto Daily *Star*, May 5, 1960 by permission of the author Pierre Berton; *Adventures of a Columnist* published by McClelland and Stewart Limited, by permission of the author Pierre Berton, © 1960; *Twenty-five Columns Twenty-five* by permission of the author, Ted Reeve; *Parade* by permission of *Maclean's* Magazine; articles in *Maclean's* Magazine by Robert Thomas Allen by permission of the author and *Maclean's* Magazine; an essay in *Wings,* September 1955, by permission of the author Eric Nicol; a column in the Toronto *Telegram,* July 26, 1965, by McKenzie Porter by permission of the Telegram Publishing Co. and the author; an article in *Maclean's* Magazine by permission of the author, McKenzie Porter; permission granted for sundry excerpts from *The Calgary Eye Opener, Questions and Answers* from *Bob Edwards' Summer Annual,* and *Eye Opener Bob* by Grant MacEwan, published by the Institute of Applied Arts, 1957, Edmonton, Alberta; *The Globe and Mail,* April 11, 1967 by permission of the author, George Bain; a column by Jim Coleman by permission of the author; radio script by Tommy Tweed by permission of the author; *Saturday Night* by permission of the author Mary Lowrey Ross; an article in *Chatelaine,* October, 1957, by John Clare by permission of the author and *Chatelaine;* a column in *The Globe and Mail,* December 1966 by permission of the author, Scott Young; an article in *Varsity,* October 18, 1939 by permission of *Varsity,* the University of Toronto; a piece in the *Goblin,* Toronto by permission of James A. Cowan; excerpts from *Behind the Beyond, The Best of Leacock, Frenzied Fiction* and *Literary Lapses* by Stephen Butler Leacock reprinted with the kind permission of McClelland and Stewart Limited, Dodd, Mead & Company Inc. and The Bodley Head; an essay in the Vancouver *Sun* July, 1957, by Barry Mather, by permission of the author and the Vancouver *Sun;* and our thanks to the Library of Parliament for the sundry excerpts from *The House of Commons Debates, Throops Scrapbook* and *More Candid Chronicles* by Hector Charlesworth; and to Jack Ayre and Alan Suddon for their help in locating material relating to the Dumbells.

Every reasonable care has been taken to make the list of acknowledgements comprehensive, but in a few cases all efforts to trace the owners of copyright have failed. It is hoped that such omissions will be pardoned.

PICTURE CREDITS

Order of appearance in the text
of pictures listed here is
left to right, top to bottom.
After the first recording,
principal sources are credited
under these abbreviations:

Sid Barron — SB
Bob Edwards' Summer Annual — BESU
Canada in Khaki — CIK
Jimmy Frise — JF
Maclean's Magazine — MM
Duncan Macpherson — DM
J W McLaren — JWM
Jack Reppen — JR
Walter Stefoff — WS
Toronto Star Syndicate — TS
Peter Whalley — PW

THE TYPE FACE USED IN THIS BOOK IS TIMES ROMAN, SET IN CANADA BY MONO LINO TYPESETTING CO. LTD.
THE BOOK WAS PRINTED AND BOUND IN ITALY BY ARNOLDO MONDADORI, OFFICINE GRAFICHE.